The Catholic Experience

LIVING FAITH

MICHAEL KEENE

STANLEY THORNES (PUBLISHERS) LTD

LIVING FAITH:
The Catholic Experience

Other books in the series:

The Christian Experience
Christianity and Social Issues

Note: Throughout the series BCE (Before Common or Christian Era) and CE (Common or Christian Era) have been used in place of the traditional BC and AD.

Biblical quotations in this book are taken from the Jerusalem Bible published by Darton, Longman and Todd, 1966.

The abbreviation 'CCC' is used to denote quotations taken from 'The Catechism of the Catholic Church' published by Geoffrey Chapman, 1994.

Text © Michael Keene 1995

Original line illustrations © Stanley Thornes (Publishers) 1995

First published in 1995 by:
Stanley Thornes (Publishers) Ltd
Ellenborough House
Wellington Street
CHELTENHAM GL50 1YD
England

A catalogue record for this book is available from the British Library

ISBN 0-7487-2189-4

Cover pictures used by permission of Andes Press Agency/Carlos Reyes

Typeset in 11/13 Galliard and Stone

Produced by AMR Ltd for Stanley Thornes (Publishers) Ltd

Printed and bound in Hong Kong

Acknowledgements

The publishers are grateful for permission to use copyright material, as follows:

Quotations from the Jerusalem Bible ©, used by permission of Darton, Longman and Todd.
Quotations from the Catechism of the Catholic Church ©, used by permission of Geoffrey Chapman – a Cassells imprint.

Also the following for permission to reproduce copyright photographs: *Andes Press Agency/Carlos Reyes:* pg 23, 25, 27, 28, 32, 33, 42, 44, 64, 66, 71, 75, 77, 80, 89, 90×2, 94, 107, 110, 122, 124, 143, 144, 147. *Hulton Dentsch:* pg 43, 70. *Hutchison Library:* pg 9, 67, 142. *Michael Keene:* pg 22, 24, 29, 133, 137. *Jo McLellan and Alex Keene:* pg 4, 5, 6, 7, 8, 10, 11, 12, 13, 15, 16, 17, 18, 19, 20, 21, 26, 30, 31, 34, 35, 36, 37, 38, 39, 40 41, 45, 48, 49, 50, 51, 52, 54, 56, 57, 58, 59, 60, 61, 65, 74, 76, 78, 79, 81, 82, 83, 84, 85, 86, 92, 93, 95, 96, 97×2, 98, 99×2, 100, 101, 102, 103, 104, 105, 108, 111, 112, 113×2, 114, 115, 116, 117, 118, 119, 120, 121×2, 123, 125, 126, 127, 128, 129, 130, 131, 132, 134, 135, 136, 138, 139, 140, 141, 145, 148, 149, 151. *Magnum Photo Library:* pg 88, 109, 152. *Mary Evans Picture Library:* pg 14, 46, 47, 53, 62, 63, 68. *Popperfoto:* pp 55, 69, 73. *Rex Features Ltd:* pg 72, 146, 150. *Telegraph Colour Library:* pg 106

The publishers have made every effort to trace the copyright holders, but if they have inadvertently overlooked any, they will be pleased to make the necessary arrangements at the first opportunity.

CONTENTS

1.1 MAN'S DESIRE FOR GOD

For men and women to be able to know and love God two very different things must take place:

a) God must have made himself known and given himself to the human race. This is called 'revelation'.

b) Men and women must respond to God by faith.

In this unit we will be looking at the ways in which God comes to meet man and the human response to that revelation through faith.

The desire for God

Man naturally desires to know and worship God. As the CCC states:

> "The desire for God is written in the human heart, because man is created by God and for God; and God never ceases to draw man to himself. Only in God will he find the truth and happiness he never stops searching for…" (27)

Throughout the centuries, to the present time, man has shown how much he desires to know and praise God through the worship that he offers – whether in the form of hymns, prayers, readings from the Holy Scriptures, sacrifices, rituals or meditations. By offering these to God man has shown that he is a religious being whilst God has demonstrated that he is close to each one of us.

Too often, men and women overlook their need for God. They forget, or even reject, the fact that they need God. Many aspects of modern life encourage this and the CCC lists some of them:

1 Religious ignorance or indifference to spiritual matters.
2 The cares and riches of this world.
3 The bad example set by many religious believers.
4 The natural reaction of sinful man to hide from God.

The news, though, is very good. Although human beings may ignore God he never ceases to call each person to follow him. Those who honestly search for God are certain to find him. The search, however, must be carried out with every effort of the mind (intellect); a sound will; an upright heart and the witness of other people who can help us to find God.

A Do you think the 'business' of life today makes it more difficult for people to spend time 'knowing' God? If so, what do you think people should do about it?

Coming to know God

Created in God's image and called by God to know and love him, human beings have found several ways of reaching God. Among them are the following:

a) Moving from the world of beauty and order to an understanding of God as the creator of the universe. It was St Paul who said:

> "For what can be known about God is perfectly plain to them since God himself has made it plain. Ever since God created the world his everlasting power and deity …have been there for the mind to see in the things he has made."
> (Romans 1.19-20)

b) Starting from the human person to a knowledge of God. The CCC highlights several aspects of human nature:
   ❖ an openness to truth and beauty;
   ❖ human freedom and the voice of the conscience;
   ❖ human longing for the infinite (God) and for happiness;
   ❖ man's concern and preoccupation with God.

Through each of these human aspects we can see that human beings have a 'soul'. The soul, 'the seed of eternity', can only have its origin in God.

B *Christians believe that everyone bears the image of God. What do you think they mean by this?*

1.2 GOD'S PLAN FOR EVERYONE

God has a plan for every human being. We could not, however, know anything about this plan unless God himself had chosen to make it known. The CCC makes this very plain:

> "God has revealed himself and given himself to man. This he does by revealing the mystery, his plan of loving goodness, formed from all eternity in Christ, for the benefit of all men." (36)

God reveals his plan

What does God want to do? He wants to give his own eternal life to all men and women. This makes us all sons and daughters of the Divine. By revealing himself to us God has made it possible for us to respond to him. God has made himself known to human beings in stages:

A If God has revealed himself plainly to the human race why do you think that so many people refuse to respond to God's revelation?

1 He made himself known 'in the beginning' through everything that he created. He invited the first people on earth, our parents, to have communion with him. Even when our parents committed their sin in the Garden of Eden (an event called 'The Fall', see Unit 2.4), God did not stop revealing himself to them.

2 Even as the human race was being wiped out by the Flood God saved Noah and his family. After the Flood, God entered into an agreement (covenant) with Noah and humanity that he would not destroy the world in future. This covenant still remains in force today.

3 To provide a focus for the whole human race God called Abraham and made him the father of a whole nation – the Jews. He released them from slavery in Egypt (a deliverance called 'The Exodus') and gave them the Law at Mount Sinai (Exodus 20). God continued to reveal himself through the many prophets who were sent by God to Israel over the following centuries. Each of them played an

important role in keeping God's revelation alive. The holiest (purest) of them all was Mary, the mother of Jesus.

4 The supreme revelation of God came through Jesus, the Word of God, who became a human being in the stable at Bethlehem. In Jesus, God has said all that needs to be said. He was the supreme revelation of God. We will find out much more about the importance of the coming of Jesus from Units 2.5 to 2.9.

With the coming of Jesus the revelation of God ended. As the CCC states:

"…there will be no other word than this one…" (65)

The Christian revelation will never pass away. No other public manifestation of God can be expected until

"…the glorious manifestation of our Lord Jesus Christ…" at the end of time.

Transmitting the revelation

This will be covered in greater detail in Unit 1.3. For the moment, we note that God has revealed himself in three ways:

a) Through the Scriptures which were written, under the inspiration of the Holy Spirit, by the Apostles and their followers.

b) Through tradition, which has been an essential part of the Church's witness through the ages.

c) Through the Church, which has a supernatural grasp on the truth and so cannot be led into error.

B How did Jesus Christ fit into God's plan?

ANSWER IN YOUR BOOK …

1 What is meant by 'revelation'?

2 What has God shared by revelation with humanity?

3 How has God revealed himself?

READ AND DECIDE …

Read this quotation from the CCC carefully:
"It pleased God, in his goodness and wisdom, to reveal himself and to make known the mystery of his will. His will was that men should have access to the Father, through Christ, the Word made flesh, in the Holy Spirit, and thus become sharers in the divine nature." (51)

a) Can you explain two ways in which God has revealed himself?

b) What do you think the phrase 'to make known the mystery of his will' means?

c) What was the will of God?

d) Why do you think that Christ is described as 'the Word made flesh'?

e) What does it mean to say that humanity have become 'sharers in the divine nature'?

CAN YOU EXPLAIN?

The writer to the Hebrews says:
"At various times in the past and in various different ways, God spoke to our ancestors through the prophets; but in our own time, the last days, he has spoken to us through his Son…" (Hebrews 1.1, 2)

a) Can you explain how God spoke in the past through his prophets?

b) Can you explain how God spoke 'in the last days' through his Son?

IN THE GLOSSARY …

Prophet; Revelation; Holy Scriptures; Holy Spirit; Apostle; Virgin Mary; Fall; Exodus; Church.

1.3 TRANSMITTING THE REVELATION

In the Epistle that he wrote to the young Church leader, Timothy, Paul wrote:

> "…he (God) wants everyone to be saved and reach (a) full knowledge of the truth."
> (1.Timothy 2.4)

The 'full knowledge of the truth' of which Paul is speaking is Jesus Christ. The Church, and every Christian believer, has the responsibility of preaching the name of Christ to every nation and making him known to all people. When this happens the 'revelation' of God is being passed on from one generation to another.

The Apostolic Tradition

Christ was the summit of God's revelation. He commanded his Apostles to preach the Gospel (the 'Good News') which was first promised by the prophets of the Old Testament and which Jesus fulfilled through his own life. Within this Gospel God's saving truth to all men and women can be found. After Jesus left the earth the Gospel was handed on and kept alive in two different ways:

1 *Orally* – by the Apostles preaching the word and passing it on to the new Christians in the communities (churches) that they had established throughout the Mediterranean area. The Gospel in this form is called the 'Oral Tradition'.
2 *In writing* – by the Apostles and others, who committed their information and beliefs about Jesus to paper. The first letters (epistles) in the New Testament were written around 50 CE whilst the first Gospel, Mark's, was penned in about 70 CE. Jesus died, we think, in about 33 CE. The truth about Jesus was preserved through the Holy Spirit.

From the Apostles to others

As the original Apostles gradually died, so bishops were appointed to take their places as leaders of the Church. The Apostles passed on to the bishops their own teaching authority. This authority was intended to be passed on from one generation to another 'until the end of time'. As we shall discover later, the authority was transferred by the 'laying on of hands' and this

tradition still finds a central place in many Catholic services.

The continual passing on of the revelation is called Tradition. We will discover more about this in Unit 1.6 but here we note two important points:

a) Through Tradition: "…the Church, in her doctrine (beliefs), life and worship, perpetuates and transmits to every generation all that she herself is, all that she believes." (CCC 78)
b) Tradition allows everything that God has revealed about himself in the past to remain present within the Church at all times.

One final point. In the remainder of this unit we will be looking at the Holy Scriptures and Tradition in some detail. We must keep in our minds the teaching of the Church that they are closely bound together. They both exist to make the mystery of Christ meaningful to the Church today and point towards the same goal at the end of time. Since the Second Vatican Council, however, the Roman Catholic Church has made it clear that the Holy Scriptures are, apart from Jesus himself, the supreme revelation of God.

A Why was the 'oral tradition' particularly important in the years following the death of Jesus?

B *Carry out some research about the part played by bishops in the modern Catholic Church. How are they appointed? What role do they play? How can they be distinguished from ordinary priests? What is the symbolism behind their distinctive dress?*

ANSWER IN YOUR BOOK ...

1 What is the main responsibility of the Church and every Christian believer?

2 What is the Christian 'Gospel'?

3 Why did it become necessary for bishops to be appointed in the early Christian Church?

CAN YOU EXPLAIN?

a) Can you explain how the revelation of God has been preserved and passed down from one generation to the next?

b) Can you explain what is meant by the 'oral tradition'? Why do you think that it was particularly important in the years following the death of Jesus?

c) After the time of the 'oral tradition' how was the message of Jesus preserved and passed on?

d) Can you explain why bishops had an important role to play in the early Church?

e) Can you explain what is meant by the 'laying on of hands'?

f) Can you explain why Tradition is important to the Catholic Church today?

g) Can you explain what the relationship is between the Holy Scriptures and Tradition?

IN THE GLOSSARY ...

Bishop; Laying on of hands; Tradition; Holy Scriptures; Epistles; St Paul; Church; Apostle; Gospel; Old Testament; Holy Spirit; Prophets; New Testament; Catholic Church.

1.4 THE HOLY SCRIPTURES (1)

The word 'bible' comes from the Latin and Greek words (biblia), which mean 'books'. This definition gives us a clue about the character of the Holy Scriptures. The Bible is not a single book but a collection of books which were brought together over a very long period of time. They were called 'holy' because they were regarded as being, in some way, inspired by God. They are 'canonical' because they are on the list 'or canon' (standard) of books which the Church regards as inspired. The official canon was settled in the 4th century although it was not solemnly recognised by the Catholic Church until the Council of Trent in 1546.

A *Why do Roman Catholics have such a high regard for the Jewish Scriptures?*

The Bible

Roman Catholics divide their Bible into three parts:

1   *The Old Testament or the Jewish Scriptures.* The early Christians were almost all Jews and they naturally turned to their own Scriptures to understand the work and ministry of Jesus. This is why the Jewish Scriptures in their entirety (the Torah, the Prophets and the Writings) are included in the Christian Bible. There are 39 books in the Old Testament altogether although the order is different in the Jewish and Christian Scriptures. All Christians regard the Old Testament as an essential part of their Scriptures. Catholics regard these Scriptures as inspired by God because:
    - ❖ the covenant (agreement) that God made with the nation of Israel, the Jews, has never been withdrawn. The Jewish people are still uniquely special to God;

- ❖ so much of the Old Testament points to the coming of Christ – a conclusion which Jews do not accept.

2   *The 'Apocrypha'.* This is the word which Protestants use to describe the Deuterocanonical books. It is a collection of texts which were omitted from the Jewish Scriptures because, although they were useful and informative, they were not considered to be inspired. When the Jewish Scriptures were translated from Hebrew into Greek in the first century CE (a translation called the Septuagint), these books were included. Jerome, who later translated from the Greek into Latin, simply continued the tradition. Modern Roman Catholic Bibles, such as the Jerusalem Bible (1966), include seven books from the Apocrypha. These are: Tobit, Judith, 1.Maccabees, 2.Maccabees, The Book of Wisdom, Ecclesiasticus and Baruch.

3   *The New Testament.* The New Testament is the holy book of Christianity. It includes stories about Jesus and teachings associated with him; the story of the founding of the early Church (the Acts of the Apostles); letters or epistles from the early Christian

leaders including John, Peter and Paul and a vision about the end of the world known as the Revelation of John (the Apocalypse). There are 27 books in the New Testament altogether. Just as the Gospels occupy a unique place in the New Testament, so they do in Catholic worship. Whereas at Mass, passages from the Old Testament and the Epistles can be read by any member of the congregation, the Gospel passage is usually read to the congregation by a deacon or a priest. Most of the Epistles in the New Testament were written before any of the Gospels. The first of these, 1.Thessalonians, was probably written by Paul in or around 49 CE. Mark's Gospel was the first to be written, between 65-70 CE, with Matthew and Luke following soon afterwards. John's Gospel was written towards the end of the 1st century.

B Can you explain why the Gospels occupy a unique place in Catholic worship?

WHAT DO YOU THINK?

a) Why do you think that the books of the Bible were thought to be 'divinely inspired' while other books around at the time were not?

b) Why do you think that Roman Catholics accept the books of the Apocrypha as part of their Holy Scriptures while Protestants do not?

c) Why do you think that all Christians accept the Jewish Scriptures as part of their own Holy Scriptures?

d) What do you think the words 'divinely inspired' mean when applied to the books in the Bible?

e) Why do you think that Christians have always looked upon the Gospels as the central part of their Scriptures?

ANSWER IN YOUR BOOK ...

1 What is the Bible?

2 What is the 'Canon of Scripture'?

3 What are the Gospels and the Epistles?

FIND OUT AND NOTE ...

Find out all that you can about the following:

a) The Apocrypha

b) The Canon of Scripture

c) The Torah

d) The Prophets

e) The Writings

IN THE GLOSSARY ...

Bible; Canon of Scripture; Council of Trent; Old Testament; Apocrypha; New Testament; Gospels; Acts of the Apostles; Roman Catholic Church; Torah; Prophets; Writings; Epistles; Revelation; Mass; Oral Tradition; Holy Scriptures; St John, St Peter; St Paul; Deacon; Priest.

The Holy Scriptures occupy a unique place in the life of the Christian Church – and that includes the Catholic Church. The Church firmly believes that:

1 God has spoken to humanity through his Son, the Divine Word, and conveyed his message to us;

2 the Bible is the sacred record of the life of Jesus;

3 the Scriptures must be held in the highest possible regard in the same way as the body and blood of Christ are respected in the Eucharist. Just as God comes to those who love him in the Mass, so he comes close to all those who read the Scriptures with faith.

God is the author of the Scriptures. He inspired the human authors of the books in the Bible to express Divine truth. This allows anyone to meet with God through reading the Scriptures. This can only happen when a person has the help and guidance of the Holy Spirit. Those who receive such guidance will discover the following:

a) The Bible's authority is unique stemming, as it does, from the inspiration of God. The Bible lays down the standards by which all other claims to truth must be judged. Both the Old and the New Testaments are equally inspired. Jesus had no hesitation in accepting the authority of the Jewish Scriptures (the Old Testament) since he quoted from them freely. Paul underlined the authority of the Old Testament when he wrote:

> "All scripture is inspired by God and can profitably be used for teaching, for refuting error, for guiding people's lives and teaching them to be holy." (2.Timothy 3.16)

From the very beginning the Church leaders saw the same inspiration in the New Testament. Put together, the whole of the Bible becomes 'God-breathed'. The entire Bible not only forms the foundation of the Church's faith but also provides everything that is needed for human salvation and forgiveness. Its authority must be accepted both within the Church and also in each individual's life.

b) The Scriptures are inerrant (without error). This does not mean that there no errors of detail or that the authors of the books did not express mistaken personal opinions. We would today, for instance, be highly critical of the Bible's acceptance of slavery as a normal fact of life. The Second Vatican Council spelt out just what the Catholic Church means when it speaks of the Scriptures being inerrant:

A What do you think people hope to gain from the public reading of the Scriptures in Church services?

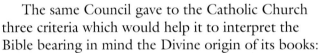

B Why do you think it is necessary for a person to have the help and guidance of the Holy Spirit before he or she can really understand what the Scriptures are saying?

"The books of Scripture must be acknowledged as teaching firmly, faithfully and without error that truth which God wanted put into the sacred writings for the sake of our salvation."

The same Council gave to the Catholic Church three criteria which would help it to interpret the Bible bearing in mind the Divine origin of its books:

❖ Although the books in the Bible are very different from each other, there is an underlying unity – of which Jesus Christ is the centre. This was made very plain after his resurrection. (Luke 24.25-27; 44-46)

❖ Scripture must be read within the tradition of the Church. Within the Church everything exists for each person to hear and understand God's Word.

❖ The Scriptures must be read with faith. They will have little to say to the person who does not have faith. This faith is a gift from God. Without it, no-one can understand God's plan for their own salvation.

CAN YOU EXPLAIN?

a) How would you explain the central position which the Scriptures occupy in the Roman Catholic Church?

b) How would you explain the sense in which Catholics believe the Scriptures to have been inspired by God?

c) How would you explain the source of the Bible's authority for Roman Catholics?

d) How would you explain what Roman Catholics mean when they describe the Bible as inerrant?

e) How would you explain the Catholic belief that the Church, and not the individual believer, is the supreme authority in understanding and interpreting the Bible?

WHAT DO YOU THINK?

What do you think that the Catholic Church means when it insists that the Scriptures can only be fully understood and interpreted by the Church?

ANSWER IN YOUR BOOK ...

1 What happens when the Bible is read and the Eucharist is celebrated?

2 What was the relationship between God and the authors of the books in the Bible?

3 How did the Second Vatican Council suggest the Bible should be approached?

IN THE GLOSSARY ...

Catholic Church; Eucharist; Bible; Holy Spirit; Old Testament; New Testament; Second Vatican Council; Holy Scriptures; Mass; St Paul.

1.6 TRADITION

As we discovered in Units 1.4 and 1.5, the Holy Scriptures stand at the very centre of Catholic belief and worship. How, though, can we be sure that the Bible is inspired? How can we be certain that the Holy Scriptures are free from doctrinal error? These are very difficult questions to answer. The New Testament makes no claim about itself. The only possible answer lies within the Church and its own traditions.

The tradition that the Bible is God's inspired book goes back to the very roots of the Christian faith in the 1st century. Over the centuries, it has been reinforced many times by various Church Councils. The Catholic believer can, therefore, accept it absolutely. In fact, one cannot be a true Catholic believer without sharing the Church's certainty over the divine origin of the Bible. It alone tells us all that we need to know about God, Christ and our personal salvation.

The Tradition

For a long time, from the Council of Trent in the 16th century onwards, the Church appeared to teach that there were two sources of Divine revelation. These are the Scriptures and Tradition. One is written (the Scriptures) and the other unwritten (Tradition). In any matters of dispute Tradition was to be given the final word.

For some time the Second Vatican Council appeared to be supporting this idea but, under the guidance of Pope John XXIII, it decided that there is just one source of truth. It may take one of two forms,

A *This print shows the earliest universal Church Council – held at Nicea in 325. Why do you think that such Councils have played such an important role in the life of the Catholic Church?*

however, and the one needs the other (Refer to **WHAT DO YOU THINK?**).

What is this tradition of which we speak? The Scriptures themselves are the product of tradition. Anyone who reads the books of the New Testament will be aware that they emerged from many sources of tradition. So there are prayers, stories which were kept alive by word of mouth or by being written down, and events which left such an impression on those who saw them that they were never forgotten.

In the centuries that followed this idea of tradition was widened. It came to mean the whole process by which the Church 'handed on' its faith to each new generation. In its widest sense it took place through preaching, teaching, devotional life, gestures (such as the sign of the cross), beliefs and the Bible itself. The tradition then became the lived, and living, faith of the Church.

Here we must be a little careful. There is *Tradition* and there are *traditions*. The faith of the Church passed down is Tradition. This is vital. The Church must always make sure that it is preserved. Traditions, though, are simply ways of doing things which have no place in the New Testament or the divinely-inspired teaching of the Catholic Church. They have proved their usefulness in the past but they can be abandoned when they no longer prove to be useful. Take, for example, the strong tradition that all priests should be celibate. There is no basis for this requirement in the New Testament and it only became part of Catholic Church life in the 12th century. Should the time come when the Church decides that celibacy is no longer necessary for the clergy, nothing essential would be lost. It is not part of the Tradition of the Church.

FIND OUT AND NOTE ...

This Roman Catholic priest has taken a vow of celibacy. No other Church makes the same demand on its clergy. Find out all that you can about celibacy. Why do you think that the demand is made? What do you think are the advantages/disadvantages of having a celibate clergy?

ANSWER IN YOUR BOOK ...

1 What is Tradition and why is it important in the Catholic Church?

2 What is the relationship between the Scriptures and Tradition?

3 What is the difference between the Tradition and tradition?

WHAT DO YOU THINK?

In one of its documents (Dogmatic Constitution on Divine Revelation) the Second Vatican Council said the following:

"It is clear that sacred tradition, sacred Scripture, and the teaching of the Church, in accord with God's most wise design, are so linked and joined together that one cannot stand without the others, and that all together and each in its own way under the action of the one Holy Spirit contribute effectively to the salvation of souls." (n.10)

a) Why do you think the question of how God speaks to people is so important?

b) Why do you think that the teaching ministry of the Church is introduced here alongside the 'sacred Tradition' and 'sacred Scripture'?

c) What does b) suggest about the individual Catholic trying to make sense of God for themselves?

d) By bringing together the Tradition, Scriptures and the Church the Second Vatican Council was trying to safeguard something. What do you think that was?

IN THE GLOSSARY ...

Bible; New Testament; Council of Trent; Pope John XXIII; Priest; Celibacy; Catholic Church; Eucharist; Holy Spirit; Old Testament; Second Vatican Council; Holy Scriptures; Church Council; Tradition; Revelation; Clergy.

1.7 FAITH

The Catholic faith is quite clear. God has spoken to men and women down the centuries through the Scriptures and the Church. He has always called men and women to be his friends – to enter into communion and fellowship with him. They can only do this, however, if they respond to this divine invitation by faith. Faith is an individual's own response to God.

What is faith?

The CCC informs us that faith is a gift from God. Peter needed this gift of faith, for example, before he could recognise Jesus as God's Messiah (Refer to READ AND DECIDE...). Such help from God does not, however, remove the simple truth that each person is free to respond to God. If they do respond they will find that the act of faith takes them beyond the power of human reason – but it does not destroy that reason. Faith is not blind. It is based upon the 'Word of God' (the Bible) which cannot be untrue.

No-one, then, is compelled to believe. The act of believing must always be a free decision. The Church repents of those times in its history when it has tried to impose the faith of the Church on others. This no longer happens.

Here are two further points about faith:

a) The Church believes that faith is necessary if someone is going to please God and have eternal life. This must be the case since human beings have been made for fellowship with God and faith is the only possible response to God.

b) Faith can be lost. The Bible tells us that only those who persevere to the end will be saved. Everyone must make sure that they do not turn away from the Faith. There are, unfortunately, millions of people who have been baptised into the Catholic faith but no longer attend church or take the sacraments.

The great example of faith

Everyone trying to live the life of faith needs an example to follow. The CCC puts forward the Blessed Virgin Mary, the mother of Jesus, as the great example of faith in God. Consider the following:

A These children have been baptised into the Catholic Church. How do you think the Church can best ensure that they remain faithful to the Church in the years to come?

B *How do you think Catholic believers try to make sure that they do not turn their backs on the Faith?*

❖ When the Angel approached Mary with the news that she was going to bear God's Son, even though she was still a virgin, Mary did not doubt that God had spoken. Instead she was convinced that:

"...nothing is impossible with God." (Luke 1.37)

❖ Mary retained her faith even when she saw Jesus crucified on the cross.

❖ Mary herself said that all generations would call her blessed' (Luke 1.48).

Finding faith

If faith is a gift from God then people cannot obtain it through their own efforts. We need help to believe in God. The only thing that we can do is to pray for the gift of faith. We can do this even if we are not sure that God exists. As Jesus himself told his disciples:

"Ask, and it will be given to you; search and you will find; knock and the door will be opened for you." (Matthew 7.7)

Even if it is God's Holy Spirit who is doing the work within us, we must work hard to open the door of faith.

ANSWER IN YOUR BOOK ...

1 What is the relationship between the revelation of God and the faith of the believer?

2 What is faith and where does it come from?

3 Why is Mary held up by Catholics as the greatest example of faith?

READ AND DECIDE ...

Here are two quotations about faith:

a) After Peter had declared that Jesus was the Messiah at Caesarea Philippi he was told by Jesus: "...it was not flesh and blood that revealed this to you but my Father in heaven." (Matthew 16.17)

b) The Second Vatican Council: "Before this faith can be exercised, man must have the grace of God to move and assist him; he must have the interior helps of the Holy Spirit, who moves the heart and converts it to God, who opens the eyes of the mind and makes it easy for all to accept and believe the truth"

❖ Why do you think that Peter could not have seen that Jesus was the Messiah without God's enlightenment?

❖ How does the quotation from the Second Vatican Council help us to understand the way that God works in those individuals who believe?

❖ Do these quotations suggest anything to you about the numerous people who do not come to believe in God?

WHAT DO YOU THINK?

In Mark 9.14-29 a father who wanted his son cured by Jesus was challenged over his faith. Read the incident through carefully. What do you think we can learn from it about faith – and lack of it?

IN THE GLOSSARY ...

Church; Messiah; Bible; Virgin Mary; St Peter; Sacrament; Holy Spirit.

The Creeds are ancient statements of belief which still sum up the doctrines and beliefs of the Catholic Church. The two Creeds which are used by the Catholic Church, the Apostles and the Nicene Creeds, can be traced all the way back to the early centuries of the Church's existence. They were drawn up by Church Councils which were mainly concerned to express what they believed about Christ – as God and man. They were forced into doing this by the teaching of heretics who were convincing many believers to hold unorthodox views. This was considered to be very dangerous for the Church's future witness and so had to be opposed.

From those early years two Creeds emerged which have played a very important part in Catholic worship ever since.

The Apostles Creed

This Creed dates back to at least 390 CE although its name might suggest that it goes all the way back to the early Apostles. Although there was a legend which suggested that this was the case, the truth appears to be that the Apostles Creed, which was first used by the Church in the 4th century, was probably based on an earlier statement of faith called the Old Roman Creed.

The old Roman Creed seems to have been used as the official baptismal Creed by the Church of Rome from the end of the 2nd century onwards, possibly even earlier. Although a link cannot be firmly established with the Apostles there is no reason to believe that their teaching was essentially different from that found in this Creed.

The Nicene Creed

This is longer than the Apostles Creed although probably later in origin. Its name suggests that it is the Creed produced by the Church at the Council of Nicea, called by the Roman Emperor Constantine in 325 CE. This was important because it was the first Church Council which had gathered together all of the Church leaders. The Nicene Creed is clearly based on that produced by the Council, although there is no clear evidence that it was regularly in use until a Mass which was celebrated at Antioch, modern Syria, in 476 CE.

What is in the Creeds?

While there are subtle differences between these two Creeds they teach essentially the same beliefs. The most important of these are the following:

a) God the Father is the Creator of the heaven and earth and everything that is in them.

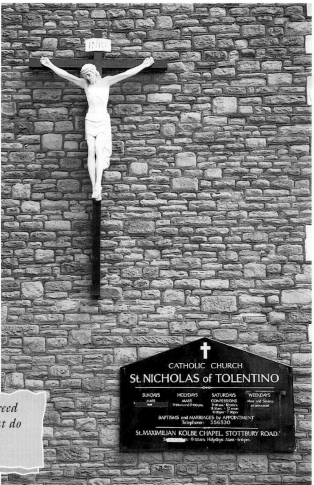

A Which words does the Nicene Creed use to describe the Church? What do you think these words mean in relation to the Church?

b) Jesus Christ, God's Son, came down from heaven to be born of the Virgin Mary. He took on human flesh, was crucified under Pontius Pilate and rose from the dead on the third day. He then ascended back into heaven. At some time in the future Jesus will return to the earth to judge those still living and bring back to life those who have died.

c) The Holy Spirit is the third member of the Trinity and is to be worshiped as such. He has spoken through the prophets and is the voice of God in the world today.

d) The Catholic Church is one, holy, catholic and apostolic. In God's sight there is just one Catholic Church, set aside as special by God. It can be found throughout the world and still continues the teaching first laid down at the beginning by the Apostles.

e) There is only one baptism within the Catholic Church which offers to all forgiveness for their sins.

f) At the end of time all will be raised from the dead and enjoy everlasting life.

Each time that the Creed is recited by members of the congregation in Catholic services the body of Christ (the Church) is indicating its commitment to the truths of the Gospel.

ANSWER IN YOUR BOOK ...

1 Where did the Apostles Creed come from?
2 What is distinctive about the Nicene Creed?
3 How would you sum up the teachings of the Apostles and Nicene Creeds?

WHAT DO YOU THINK?

Do you think that it would make a tremendous difference to the authority of the Apostles Creed if that Creed could be traced all the way back to the original Apostles of Jesus?

CAN YOU EXPLAIN?

This stained glass window shows Mary and the baby Jesus. Here are some quotations from the Nicene Creed about Jesus Christ. Can you explain what you think they mean?

a) "We believe in one Lord, Jesus Christ, the only Son of God, eternally begotten of the Father..."

b) "For us men and for our salvation he came down from heaven: by the power of the Holy Spirit he became incarnate from the Virgin Mary, and was made man."

c) "On the third day he rose again..."

d) "He will come again in glory to judge the living and the dead."

IN THE GLOSSARY ...

Creed; Catholic Church; Church Council; Heretic; Apostles Creed; Nicene Creed; Mass; Apostle; Virgin Mary; Holy Spirit; Trinity; Prophet; Baptism; Gospel.

2.2 GOD, THE FATHER ALMIGHTY

As the Nicene Creed begins with the fundamental statement – "I believe in the one God" – so we encounter the basis for the Roman Catholic Church's belief about God. The oneness of God (a belief called monotheism) is firmly rooted in the Old Testament, where Israel acknowledged that there was one God who must be worshipped with the whole heart, soul and strength. This faith was confirmed by Jesus (Refer to **READ AND DECIDE…**).

From this foundation other beliefs about God develop:

a) *That God alone is.* There are no other gods and he is beyond the world and time. As the Psalmist wrote:

> "Aeons ago, you laid the earth's foundations,
> the heavens are the work of your hands;
> all will vanish, though you remain,
> all wear out like a garment,
> like clothes that need changing you will change them;
> but yourself, you never change, and your years are unending."
> (Psalm 102. 25-27)

Everyone depends on someone else for their existence. God is the one exception.

b) *That God is a Holy Trinity.* The revelation of the Trinity was expressed in the baptismal faith and practice of the early Church. It was part of its preaching, prayer and teaching. The Nicene and Apostles Creeds expressed this in the language of the time. There are not three Gods – only one God in three persons. Father, Son and Holy Spirit do not share the one divinity, Each one of them is fully God and yet there is only one God.

c) *That God is the creator of the world.* Catholic belief does not reject the theory of evolution. Science answers the question 'What kind of world do we live in?' The Biblical story of creation answers the question 'Why is there a world of any kind in which to live?' Everything that we discover about the natural world should increase our sense of wonder and awe. Creation was the work of the Trinity:

❖ "In the beginning God created the heaven and the earth." (Genesis 1.1)
❖ "In the beginning was the Word (Jesus)…He was with God in the beginning. Through him all things came to be…" (John 1.1,2)
❖ The Holy Spirit is the 'Creator Spiritas' (Creator Spirit) – as the Church affirms in its worship.

A *How would you explain to the parents of this baby that God is its creator?*

d) *That God has revealed himself to the world.* God is unknowable and left to our own devices we would know nothing about him. As we will discover in Unit 2.4 the Catholic Church believes in the Fall, the first act of disobedience committed in the Garden of Eden, which has left the human race with a strong tendency to be sinful. Yet God, in his love, has chosen to reveal himself to humanity. In sending his only Son, Jesus Christ, and the Holy Spirit, God has shown his love for us. Talking of God revealing himself should remind us that the God of the Christians is 'hidden'. Though we can, and should, go a long way towards God through our reason, God is 'beyond' reason. As St Paul writes:

"Now we see in a mirror
dimly…"
(1.Corinthians 13.12)
"…we walk by faith and not by
sight." (2.Corinthians 5.7)

Genuine Catholics are those people who are walking by faith, and not by sight!

B *When you see love last and flourish between two human beings, what does that teach you about the love of God?*

ANSWER IN YOUR BOOK …

1 What is the basic belief about God on which all other beliefs are built?

2 What is the Shema?

3 What is the Trinity?

READ AND DECIDE …

We read these words in Mark 12.29,30. A scribe has asked Jesus which is the greatest of all the commandments and he replies:

"This is the first, Listen, Israel, the Lord our God is the one Lord, and you must love the Lord your God with all your heart, with all your soul, with all your mind, and with all your strength. The second is this: You must love your neighbour as yourself."

a) The first part of the answer of Jesus is almost a direct quote from the great Jewish statement of belief – the Shema. You can find this in Deuteronomy 6.4-5. What change did Jesus make to this statement? Can you suggest any reason why he did so?

b) Why do you think Jesus linked loving God with loving one's neighbour?

FIND OUT AND NOTE …

In the 'Profession of Faith of Pope Paul VI' we read these words:

"We believe in one God, Son and Holy Spirit, creator of things visible – such as this world in which our brief life runs its course – and of things invisible – such as the pure spirits which are also called angels."

In this quotation we meet a straightforward statement of the Catholic belief in angels. Can you find out what Catholics believe about angelic beings?

IN THE GLOSSARY …

Nicene Creed; Roman Catholic Church; Trinity; Apostles Creed; Holy Spirit; Old Testament; Fall.

2.3 HUMAN BEINGS

The CCC summarises its teaching about human beings in the following way:

1 God has made man in his own image and likeness. For this reason, man occupies a unique place in the world of creation.
2 Man, in his nature, unites the spiritual and the material worlds.
3 God has created human beings, male and female.
4 God has set up a unique relationship, one of friendship, between himself and human beings.

The Image of God

The CCC is quite clear. Of all the creatures in the world:

> "…only man is able to know and love his creator." (356)

Man alone has been called to share in God's own life. By being made in God's image man is a 'person' – not just a something but a someone. Man is capable of self-knowledge, self-possession and of freely giving himself to and entering into fellowship with other human beings. Most important of all, human beings are called to enter into a relationship with their Creator – an invitation that is not extended to any other form of life. God has created everything for man. In return, man has been created to serve God and 'to offer all creation back to him.' (CCC 358)

If human beings really want to know why God has created them they must look at Jesus since it is only:

> "…in the mystery of the Word made flesh (Jesus) that the mystery of man becomes clear." (CCC 359)

Adam and Christ

St Paul tells us that the human race owes its origins to two men: Adam (the first man) and Christ (called the second Adam). Christ, the great Creator, gave life to Adam and stamped his own image on him. When that 'image' was lost through the sin in the Garden of Eden the second Adam (Christ) came into the world to bring God's forgiveness and healing. Adam had a beginning and an end. The second Adam had no beginning and does not end.

The human race shares a common origin in Adam. We are all brothers and sisters of each other:

a) We share the same unity of nature since we are all composed of body and soul.
b) We share the same blessings of the earth which is able to sustain and develop all life.
c) We share the same salvation which Christ himself died to give us.

This does not mean to say, of course, that we are all completely the same. One of the glories of life is its diversity, the rich variety of persons, cultures and peoples. Indeed, such diversity is a guarantee that all people are truly united with one another.

A When we speak of these children carrying the 'image of God' what are we trying to say about them?

The soul

In the second account of creation (Genesis 2) we read the following:

> "Yahweh (God) fashioned man of dust from the soil. Then he breathed into his nostrils a breath of life, and thus man became a living being (soul)."
> (Genesis 2.7)

Human beings alone are (have) souls. The 'soul' is the innermost part of a human being, that which is most valuable. The soul indicates that which is most obviously the 'image of God'. Put another way, the 'soul' indicates the 'spiritual principle' in man.

B *How important are the differences in the human family and how do these underline the essential unity of the human race?*

ANSWER IN YOUR BOOK ...

1 Why does the human race occupy a unique place in creation?

2 What is unique about the relationship which exists between God and human beings?

3 What did St Paul mean when he spoke of the 'first Adam' and the 'second Adam'?

WHAT DO YOU THINK?

The Catholic understanding of man places its emphasis on his uniqueness. Think about this carefully. Can you think of five ways in which human beings are essentially different from all other forms of life? What do you think it is that makes men and women the people that they are?

CAN YOU EXPLAIN?

a) Can you explain just what the CCC teaches about human beings?

b) Can you explain just what is meant by saying that human beings are made in the 'image of God'?

c) Can you explain what the CCC means when it speaks of human beings offering creation back to God?

d) Can you explain what is meant when we speak of the unity of the human race?

e) Can you explain the relationship between the 'first Adam' and the 'second Adam'?

f) Can you explain what is meant by the 'soul'?

IN THE GLOSSARY ...

St Paul; Soul.

2.4 THE FALL

The Catholic Church believes that there are three truths which could only be known if God had revealed them to us:

a) That in the beginning, the first man and woman lived in the paradise of the Garden of Eden.

b) That their world was perfect until the couple first succumbed to temptation and fell into sin. This event, called the 'Fall', belongs to the earliest time in humanity's history.

c) That the Gospel (the Good News) shows us Jesus, who is offered as the Saviour of all. Those who respond to this offer of salvation are the 'redeemed' – those 'bought back' from the slavery of sin. We will find out more about this in Unit 2.9.

A What do you think it really means to say that we are all 'tainted with sin' from the moment we are born?

Here we are concerned to discover just what the Church believes about sin.

Original Sin

The account of the fall of the first man and woman into sin, Genesis 3, uses:

> "...figurative language, but affirms a primeval event..." (CCC 390)

The CCC is making a very important point. The Fall took place at the very beginning of the history of the human race. It cannot be dated but it is essential to see it as a historical event. Revelation also teaches us that the whole of human history has been affected by the consequences of that first sinful act of disobedience. In the beginning, God created man in his image and everything was perfect. That perfection has been lost for ever.

What was this sin really about? In the first paradise the man and the woman were free to make their own choices but God laid one restriction on them. They found that restriction irksome (Genesis 3.1-7). They wanted to be in total control of their own destiny. As a consequence, they made the fateful choice to disobey God. Immediately, their eyes were opened to see a new world but the consequences of their actions have been with us ever since. Instead of the perfection which they found in the Garden of Eden they began to experience a world of disharmony, pain, suffering and death.

The first parents could not help but pass on this tendency to sin to all their descendants down to the present day. Roman Catholics call it 'concupiscence'. The sin is forgiven through baptism but this sacrament cannot remove the sinful tendency. Human beings constantly feel the pressure of temptation to sin.

The 'Evil One'

Who exerts this pressure of temptation on us? John provides us with the answer:

> "...the whole world lies in the power of the Evil One." (1.John 5.19)

24

Talking of the 'Evil One' leads us to understand just what lay behind the first disobedience in the Garden of Eden. Both Scripture and Church tradition identify the seductive voice of temptation as belonging to Satan (the Devil), a fallen angel. As the Lateran Council of 1215 taught:

> "The devil and the other demons were indeed created naturally good by God but they became evil by their own doing."

The Scriptures tell us that the Devil has 'sinned from the beginning … he is a Liar and the father of lies' (1.John 3.8; John 8.44). At the very beginning of the ministry of Jesus the Devil tried to tempt him into taking the easy path. According to the CCC, the greatest mystery of all is that God allowed, and continues to allow, such diabolical behaviour but the Christian knows that 'in everything God works for good with those who love him.' (Romans 8.28)

In fact, through the death of Jesus, God restricted the activities of Satan. In the end, Satan will be destroyed and God's Kingdom will be established for ever.

B *A modern South American sculpture of the snake tempting Eve in the Garden of Eden. What do you think the Catholic Church means when it says that every human being has a tendency to sin from the moment they are born?*

ANSWER IN YOUR BOOK …

1 What do Roman Catholics mean when they speak of 'The Fall'?

2 What is meant by 'Original Sin'?

3 What is 'concupiscence'?

READ AND DECIDE …

Here are two quotations from the CCC. Read them through carefully:

a) "Satan or the devil and the other demons are fallen angels who have freely refused to serve God and his plan. Their choice against God is definitive. They try to associate man in their revolt against God." (414)

  ❖ What does the word 'Satan' mean?
  ❖ What does the phrase 'fallen angels' mean?
  ❖ What divine plan is being referred to here?
  ❖ How would you explain the phrase 'Their choice against God is definitive.'
  ❖ How did the demons try 'to associate man in their revolt against God'?

b) "Adam and Eve transmitted to their descendants human nature wounded by their own first sin and hence deprived them of original holiness and justice…" (414)

  ❖ When did Adam and Eve commit the 'first sin'?
  ❖ What is the belief that the whole of humanity has been affected by the first sin called?
  ❖ What has humanity lost as a result of the first sin?

IN THE GLOSSARY …

Fall; Gospel; Original Sin; Baptism; Holy Scriptures; Satan; Sacrament; Devil.

2.5 JESUS CHRIST – HIS INCARNATION

The Incarnation (the birth of God as a human being) is the greatest mystery of the Christian religion. Catholics believe that Jesus became man to take away the sins of the human race and to openly demonstrate to everyone the love of God. He now invites men and women to become his disciples and so share in his divine nature.

Jesus

The angel announced the birth of Jesus to Joseph with the words:

> "You shall call his name Jesus, for he will save his people from their sins." (Matthew 1.21)

There are two great acts of 'salvation' in the Bible:

1 When the Children of Israel were slaves in Egypt God saved them and led them into a new Promised Land (called Canaan). This event, known as the Exodus, is still celebrated annually by Jews in their festival of the Passover.
2 God now saves his people, the Church, from their enslavement to sin. Jesus (God saves) came to show salvation and forgiveness through his own death and resurrection.

The word 'Christ' is the Greek translation of the Hebrew word 'Messiah', meaning 'anointed'. Jesus was sent by God to bring salvation to everyone who believes. The story began when Jesus, existing with God from eternity, was born as a human being into a stable in Bethlehem. That is the 'Incarnation'.

God and man

The Christian Church has always maintained two important beliefs about Jesus. He is believed to be:

a) *Fully divine – the Son of God.* From time to time, during his earthly life, the divinity of Jesus became apparent – albeit, only briefly. One such occasion was the transfiguration of Jesus (Luke 9.28-36) which followed hard on Peter's great declaration about Jesus at Caesarea Philippi. The transfiguration looked forward to the glory which Jesus was going to share after his resurrection from the dead. It also highlighted the Christian believer's own transfiguration when Jesus will:

> "...transfigure our lowly bodies and make them like his own." (Philippians 3.21)

A Why do you think that Paul calls the Incarnation the mystery which stands at the centre of the Christian Faith?

b) *Fully human.* The Incarnation is all about the birth of God. Mary is the mother of this divine person so she can be called the 'Mother of God' – the 'Theotokos'. This will be discussed further in Units 2.11 and 2.12.

Throughout the Gospels Jesus demonstrated that he was fully human. He was hungry; he was angry; he was upset; he loved others and he was disappointed when others let him down. As the writer to the Hebrews put it:

> "For it is not as if we had a high priest who was incapable of feeling our weaknesses with us; but we have one who was tempted in every way that we are, though he is without sin."
> (Hebrews 4.15)

In Jesus, Catholics see both the Son of God and the Son of Man. His divinity and his humanity are equally important. Without being divine he could not have secured our salvation. Without being human he could not have fully shared our trials and tribulations. Being totally divine and totally human he is the perfect Saviour. It is this that Paul was referring to when he wrote that "the mystery of our religion is very deep indeed".

B When Catholics think about Jesus what kind of figure do you think they have in mind?

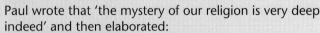

ANSWER IN YOUR BOOK …

1 What is meant by the 'Incarnation'?
2 What is the significance of the name 'Jesus'?
3 What does the title 'Christ' mean?

TO THINK ABOUT …

Paul wrote that 'the mystery of our religion is very deep indeed' and then elaborated:
> "He was made visible in the flesh,
> attested by the Spirit,
> seen by angels,
> proclaimed to the pagans,
> believed in by the world,
> taken up in glory."
> (1.Tim 3.16)

There are six phrases here which, according to Paul, sum up the earthly life of Jesus. Can you come up with as many examples as possible from the life of Jesus to illustrate each of these phrases?

READ AND DECIDE …

The Jewish historian, Josephus, wrote his great work 'The Antiquities of the Jews' in 77 CE. Concerning Jesus he wrote:
> "It was at that time that a man appeared – if 'man' is the right word – who had all the attributes of a man but seemed to be something greater. His actions, certainly, were superhuman for he worked such wonderful and amazing miracles that I cannot for one regard him as a man; yet in view of his likeness to ourselves I cannot regard him as an angel either."

How has the Catholic Church dealt with the tension between the divine and the human attributes of Jesus?

IN THE GLOSSARY …

Incarnation; Exodus; Passover; Messiah; Church; Gospels; Virgin Mary.

27

2.6 THE MINISTRY OF JESUS

We know very little about the early years of Jesus – a time which the CCC calls the 'hidden life at Nazareth' (533). In fact, after Jesus has returned to Nazareth from Egypt with his parents at the age of two, only one reference is made to his childhood. This is to tell us of the time when Jesus visited the Temple in Jerusalem during the Passover festival (Luke 2.41-5). The importance of this occasion lies in the clear reference which Jesus made to his future life's mission – his 'father's business'.

The baptism and temptation

A *How does the Catholic Church try to follow the example of Jesus when he was baptised?*

Around the age of thirty Jesus emerged from obscurity to be baptised by John the Baptist in the River Jordan (Luke 3.23). After being baptised the Holy Spirit, in the form of a dove, sat upon the shoulders of Jesus as a voice from heaven declared:"

> "You are my Son, the Beloved; my favour rests on you." (Luke 3.22)

The baptism of Jesus was significant in three ways:

1 The other two members of the Trinity, God the Father and God the Holy Spirit, identified themselves with the future ministry of Jesus. In all that he said and did he was representing the whole Trinity.

2 By being baptised along with those who had come to confess their sins, Jesus was identifying himself with the human race. We already begin to see him as:

> "…the Lamb of God who takes away the sins of the world…" (John 1.29)

3 Jesus was providing us all with an example to follow. At an early stage in the Church's history baptism came to be the way in which all believers could identify themselves with the humility of Jesus.

The Gospels agree that, as soon as the baptism was completed, Jesus was driven by the Spirit into the wilderness to be tempted three times by Satan (Luke 4.13).

This recalls two events in the Old Testament:

a) The temptation of Adam in the Garden of Eden.

b) The temptations of the Israelites in the wilderness on their way to the Promised Land.

The public Jesus

Soon after the baptism of Jesus, John the Baptist was arrested by King Herod. At the same time Jesus began preaching to the people:

> "The time has come and the Kingdom of God is close at hand. Repent, and believe the Good News." (Mark 1.15)

Most of his subsequent teaching was taken up with God's Kingdom (see Unit 2.7) and Jesus accompanied this teaching with 'many mighty works and wonders and signs' to underline that he was God's promised Messiah – as you will discover in Unit 2.8. Jesus also freed people from the evils of hunger, injustice, illness and death and these were also 'signs' to show that he was someone very special. The greatest 'sign' of all, however, was the power that Jesus had to set people free from their sins (John 8.34-36). To do this he had to wage war with Satan. As Jesus said to those who opposed his ministry:

> "…if it is through the Spirit of God that I cast devils out, then know that the Kingdom of God has overtaken you." (Matthew 12.26,28)

Throughout his ministry Jesus was accompanied by the twelve men that he had chosen at the outset to be his closest friends – and disciples (Mark 3.13-19). He gave them a share in his own authority and also sent them out, two by two, to preach and heal. To begin with three of the disciples, Peter, James and John, emerged as the 'inner circle' but towards the end Peter was clearly the leader. You will find out more about him and his subsequent importance to the Catholic Church in Unit 3.9.

B How do you think the work of this doctor might be seen in the context of the battle between good and evil?

ANSWER IN YOUR BOOK …

1 What was the significance of the baptism of Jesus?
2 Which two events in the Old Testament are brought to mind by the temptations of Jesus?
3 What great theme did Jesus introduce in his ministry?

READ AND DECIDE …

Read Luke 2.41-52 carefully before answering these questions:

a) What was the festival of the Passover and which event in Jewish history did it commemorate?
b) Why do you think that Jesus was to be found sitting among the 'doctors' asking them questions?
c) How do you understand the reply of Jesus when he was challenged by his parents about staying behind in Jerusalem?
d) Why do you think that Luke says that Jesus returned to Nazareth with his parents and 'lived under their authority'? What point do you think he was trying to make by this comment?
e) Can you explain the significance of the statement: "Jesus increased in wisdom, in stature and in favour with God and men." (Luke 2.52).

FIND OUT AND NOTE …

Jesus saw his own ministry in terms of a conflict between the powers of darkness and himself. Can you find out whether the Catholic Church believes in the existence of such evil powers today? If so, what authority do such powers have and what evidence is suggested for their activity in the modern world?

IN THE GLOSSARY …

Passover; Holy Spirit; Trinity; Baptism; Satan; Old Testament; Kingdom of God; Messiah; Disciple; St Peter; St John; Catholic Church.

2.7 THE TEACHING OF JESUS

We find the substance of the teaching of Jesus in the first three Gospels – Matthew, Mark and Luke. Together these are called the 'Synoptic Gospels': from the Greek word 'synopsis' meaning 'seeing together'. The Catholic Church believes that these Gospels are essentially trustworthy records of the teaching of Jesus. Matthew tells us that Jesus taught the people 'with authority' (Matthew 7.29) and it is this authority which marks out the teaching of Jesus in the Gospels as distinctive.

The Law and Traditions

The teaching of Jesus fitted into the traditions already established by the Jewish teachers (rabbis) of the past. They interpreted God's Torah (usually translated 'Law' but better translated 'Teaching') for the people. Jesus accepted the teachings of the Torah, found in the first five books of the Jewish Scriptures, as he indicated clearly by saying:

> "Do not imagine that I have come to abolish the Law or the Prophets. I have come not to abolish but to complete them. I tell you solemnly, till heaven and earth disappear, not one dot, not one little stroke, shall disappear from the Law until its purpose is achieved." (Matthew 5.17,18)

The problem that Jesus had was not with the Torah itself but with the many traditions that had sprung up around it. Jesus believed that the heart of the Torah mattered far more than the individual laws. When asked by a scribe to identify the most important of the Torah's many commandments he replied:

> "Listen, Israel, the Lord our God is one Lord, and you must love the Lord your God with all your heart, with all your soul, with all your mind and with all your strength' (Mark 12.29,30)

He also said:

> "You must love your neighbour as yourself." (Mark 12.20)

These two quotations, from Deuteronomy 6.4,5 and Leviticus 19.18, sum up the whole teaching of Jesus.

A *What do you think makes a good teacher? What do you think were the characteristics which marked out the teaching of Jesus as memorable?*

The Kingdom of God

All four Gospels linked the early ministry of Jesus with that of John the Baptist. There was a good reason for this. Both of them told the people that the Kingdom (reign) of God was 'close at hand' (Matthew 3.2 and 4.17) but Jesus went on to indicate that the kingdom had actually arrived.

The 'good news' of this kingdom was the love and peace which Jesus came to share with men and women. Jesus offered God's mercy to all who responded to him as his actions showed. He extended it to those who were outcasts in society – Roman soldiers, tax collectors, prostitutes, Samaritans and the poor among others. They were the people that Jesus welcomed into God's kingdom ahead of the others. The 'Beatitudes', in Matthew 5.1-12, describe the characteristics shown by those who become members of the kingdom. This was also displayed in many of the parables that Jesus told such as the Lost Son (Luke 15.11-32) and the Good Samaritan (Luke 10.29-37).

The task of the Catholic Church today is to continue the ministry of Jesus in proclaiming the Kingdom of God. It does this when it preaches the Gospel of Christ. It also does so when it shows the love of Christ in its dealings with people from all different nations, racial backgrounds and social conditions. This is the true mission of the Catholic Church.

ANSWER IN YOUR BOOK …

1 What are the Synoptic Gospels and why are they so-called?

2 What is the Torah and what was the attitude of Jesus towards it?

3 What was the 'Kingdom of God'?

CAN YOU EXPLAIN?

You will find the Beatitudes in Matthew 5.1-12. They explain the characteristics of those people who are part of God's Kingdom – often without knowing it. Read them through carefully before answering these questions:

a) Why do you think that the Beatitudes have been called the 'Magna Carta' of Christianity?

b) The Beatitudes pick out eight groups of people who all exhibit highly desirable spiritual characteristics. The meaning of some of these characteristics is straightforward but can you try to explain the following:
   ❖ "How happy are the poor in spirit." (v.3)
   ❖ "Happy those who mourn". (v.5)
   ❖ "Happy those who hunger and thirst for what is right." (v.6)
   ❖ "Happy the merciful." (v.7)
   ❖ "Happy the pure in heart." (v.8)
   ❖ "Happy those who are persecuted in the cause of right." (v.10)

c) Some of the rewards offered belong to the life to come and some are given in this life. Why do you think this distinction is made?

B Why do you think that Jesus placed such emphasis upon loving one's neighbour as well as loving God?

IN THE GLOSSARY …

Gospels; Synoptic Gospels; Catholic Church; Rabbi; Torah; Kingdom of God; Parable.

2.8 THE MIRACLES OF JESUS

Writing towards the end of the first century Josephus, the Jewish historian, referred to Jesus as a 'miracle-worker'. This seemed to have been accepted by almost everyone at the time. Few people questioned that he healed the sick; fed the hungry; calmed the storms; cast out demons and raised the dead. Even his enemies recognised that Jesus had extraordinary power and authority. They knew that he could not have done such things unless he had help and power from 'outside'.

The whole debate was about the source of that power. His followers were convinced that the miracles of Jesus were a clear sign that God's reign on earth had begun. The only possible explanation was that God was active within him. His enemies, however, were equally sure that the miracles had been performed by another power altogether: that of Satan or 'Beelzebub', as the Devil was then called. Jesus replied that this suggestion was quite absurd – how could Satan cast out his own evil spirits (Matthew 12.24)?

The Catholic Church and miracles

The First Vatican Council, called by Pope Pius IX in 1870, had some strong words to say about the following:

❖ Anyone who says that miracles cannot happen.
❖ Anyone who says that the miracles in the Bible are no more than 'fable and myth'.
❖ Anyone who says that it is never possible to establish with certainty that a miracle has taken place.
❖ Anyone who insists that miracles do not prove the divine origin of the Christian faith.

The Council recommended that these people should be excommunicated (barred from the Church's sacraments).

There are many recorded miracles in the Gospels. They fall into three categories:

a) *Miracles of nature* – Christ walking on water, calming a storm etc.

A *Lourdes has been thought to be a 'healing centre' since the middle of the 19th century. The Church authorities, however, have been very cautious about making such claims. Can you find out how the Church attempts to verify any claims that are made about a miracle having taken place at this holy site?*

b) *Miracles of healing* – Christ curing a blind man, healing a deaf and dumb man etc.

c) *Miracles of raising the dead* – Christ brought Lazarus and a young boy back to life.

Concerning these miracles, it is important to say that they rarely took place without faith being involved. Jesus almost always linked his willingness to perform a miracle with the faith of the person in need or, on some occasions, with the faith of others. When four men brought a paralytic to Jesus to be healed, for example, it was their faith which Jesus saw and respected (Mark 2.5).

The Catholic Church today teaches that people should pray for healing of the body, mind and spirit – for themselves and for others. It is God's will that we are all whole. Yet sickness and suffering can also be part of God's will for us. Sickness is important because it allows our faith to be tested and strengthened. Learning to be patient in prayer leads to an inner healing of the spirit, even if our outward physical condition remains unaltered.

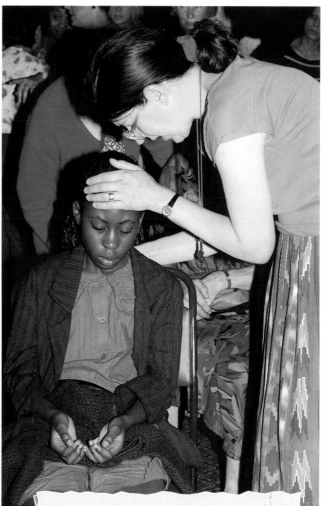

B Do you see any danger in meetings like this which offer healing to people who come?

ANSWER IN YOUR BOOK …

1 What did everyone, friend and enemy alike, acknowledge about Jesus and his miracles?

2 How did the enemies of Jesus seek to explain his miracles?

3 What is 'excommunication'.

IN YOUR OWN WORDS …

a) Can you explain the attitude of the First Vatican Council towards those who denied that miracles could take place? Why do you think that its condemnation was so strong?

b) Into which three separate categories do the miracles of Jesus fall? Do you find all of the miracles of Jesus equally easy, or difficult, to believe? Explain your answer.

c) Why do you think that Jesus almost always demanded some evidence of faith before he was prepared to perform a miracle? Do you think the miracles were performed because of the faith of the people? Could there have been another reason?

d) How do you think the Church should continue the 'healing' ministry of Christ today? Do you think that people are still being healed through the Church's ministry? If so, why is it that many people who have prayed for healing have still not received it?

READ AND DECIDE …

These three passages describe very different miracles performed by Jesus:

a) Matthew 9.32-34.

b) John 11.1-44.

c) Luke 9.10-17.

Read them through carefully and write up your own description of each event. To what extent is the faith of the people involved said to be important?

IN THE GLOSSARY …

Satan; Devil; Catholic Church; First Vatican Council; Bible; Gospels; Excommunication.

2.9 JESUS CHRIST – HIS DEATH AND RESURRECTION

As we saw in Unit 2.4, the relationship between God and human beings was greatly affected by the Fall. The very roots of human nature were damaged by the sin of our first parents. Left to our own devices we are helpless. Catholics believe, however, that they have been saved from the consequences of sin by the death of Jesus on Calvary and by his resurrection from the dead. God's forgiveness is now freely available to all those who believe in Christ.

The death of Jesus

The death of Jesus on the cross stands at the centre of the Catholic faith. Anyone who enters a Catholic church soon becomes aware of this. Around the walls the Stations of the Cross (a series of 14 pictures or sculptures) trace the last few hours in the life of Jesus. Crucifixes, on the altar and elsewhere, reinforce the message that this is the foundation on which Catholicism stands or falls.

The New Testament does not provide a detailed explanation of the link between the Fall, the death of Jesus and forgiveness by God. Instead, it provides us with a series of pictures which fit together like pieces of a jigsaw. It teaches that:

a) Jesus is our example. When Jesus accepted his suffering and death, after his anguish in the Garden of Gethsemane, he provided everyone with an example to follow. God's own Son did not shrink from the consequences of being human. He accepted the pain that is so much a part of the human condition. We can learn from him and be stirred by his example.

b) Jesus triumphed over the powers of darkness by his death. When Jesus died sin and death (the powers of darkness) were locked in mortal combat with love and life (the light of the Gospel). In that moment the powers of evil fired their final weapon against God – and failed. The resurrection of Jesus from the dead is the proof that the final victory belonged to God.

A *The Stations of the Cross, found in every Catholic church, tell the story of the events leading up to the death of Jesus. Can you identify what is happening in this embroidered Station of the Cross?*

c) Jesus reconciled (brought together) God and the human race by his death. Because of sin, human beings could not enjoy any kind of relationship with God. Throughout the Old Testament man struggled to establish a relationship with God by offering sacrifices. The attempt failed. The death of Jesus changed all that. As a human being he represented humanity while as God, he alone could pay the full price of sin. This underlines the Catholic belief that, while God is loving, he is also just and cannot simply overlook sin.

d) By allowing his Son to die, God provided us with the supreme example of total, self-giving love. In allowing himself to be nailed to the cross, Jesus showed us the true cost of resigning ourselves completely to the will of God.

e) Jesus was a sacrifice. By dying, the blameless Jesus offered himself as the perfect sacrifice to God. He became the Lamb of God who takes away the sins of the world. By substituting his obedience for our disobedience, Jesus allowed us to share in his sacrifice. This we do each time we participate in the Mass.

The only way to really understand the death of Jesus is to bring all of these 'pictures' together into one whole picture and then enter into that death through the celebration of the Mass. The Mass is the continual re-offering of the sacrifice of Christ.

The resurrection of Christ from the dead? Where does that fit in? The CCC provides us with the answer:

> "The Resurrection above all constitutes the confirmation of all Christ's works and teachings. All truths, even those most inaccessible to human reason, find their justification if Christ by his resurrection has given the definitive proof of his divine authority, which he had promised." (651)

The resurrection of Christ, brought about by the power of God, sets the seal on all that he taught and did. His whole ministry was justified and accepted by God, as the resurrection demonstrates. If the powers of darkness could not keep the body of Christ in the tomb then those powers will not be able to exert power over human beings either. The resurrection shows that the power of Satan has been finally broken.

B *Crucifixes are common features of Catholic churches and spirituality. Why do you think that so many Catholics find crucifixes an enormous help in their devotional lives?*

ANSWER IN YOUR BOOK ...

1 What is the relationship between the Fall and the death of Jesus on Calvary?

2 How is the central importance of the crucifixion shown in every Roman Catholic church?

3 What was changed as a result of the crucifixion? What pictures are used in the New Testament to describe this change?

WRITE AN ESSAY ...

As you discovered in the text, the New Testament uses many pictures to explain the death of Jesus. Keep them in mind as you read the following references:

1.Corinthians 15.3; 1.John 4.10; 2.Corinthians 5.19; Luke 22.19; Matthew 20.28; John 3.16; John 13.1.

Now write an essay of about 500 words on the subject 'The Meaning of the Death of Jesus'.

CAN YOU EXPLAIN?

Here are three quotations from the New Testament. Read each of them through carefully:

a) "As he (Christ) is the beginning,
he was first to be born from the dead,
so that he should be first in every way;
because God wanted all perfection
to be found in him
and all things to be reconciled through him and for him,
everything in heaven and everything on earth,
when he made peace
by his death on the cross." (Colossians 1.18)

b) "...when we were baptised we went into the tomb with him and joined him in death, so that as Christ was raised from the death by the Father's glory, we too might live a new life." (Romans 6.4)

c) "...if the Spirit of him who raised Jesus from the dead is living in you, then he who raised Jesus from the dead will give life to your own mortal bodies through his Spirit living in you." (Romans 8.11)

Can you explain the link which Paul sees between the resurrection of Jesus from the dead and the future resurrection of all Christian believers?

IN THE GLOSSARY ...

Stations of the Cross; Crucifix; Fall; Gospel; Mass; Satan; New Testament.

2.10 THE HOLY SPIRIT

The Roman Catholic Church is totally committed to its belief in the Trinity – God the Father, God the Son and God the Holy Spirit. The order in which they are presented above, and in worship, does not represent an order of importance. It simply indicates the order in which the three persons of the Trinity have been revealed:

a) God the Father created the world.

b) God the Son was revealed through the Incarnation and given the task of redeeming the world.

c) God the Holy Spirit, although present in both creation and the Incarnation, is primarily the 'paraclete' (advocate) who was promised by Jesus and perfectly revealed on the Day of Pentecost. He continues to be God-in-action in the world today.

Symbols of the Holy Spirit

Throughout the New Testament symbols or images are provided to help us to understand the work carried out by the Holy Spirit. Among them are the following:

1 *Water.* This signifies the work of the Holy Spirit in baptism, which is the sign of 'new birth'. Just as our first birth took place in water so our second birth (our spiritual rebirth) also takes place through water. This time, it is the water of baptism. As 1.Corinthians 12.13 reminds us, 'by one Spirit we were all baptised' so we are all made to 'drink of the one Spirit'.

2 *Anointing.* It was the task of the prophet in the Old Testament to 'anoint' God's choice as Israel's king with oil to show that they had been 'set apart' for their God-given task. In the New Testament the symbolism of anointing with oil referred to the gift of the Holy Spirit and this is retained in the sacraments of ordination and confirmation.

3 *Fire.* Fire symbolises the transforming power of God's actions in the believer as well as the purifying activity of God within the human heart. It was as 'tongues of fire' that the Holy Spirit possessed the first Christians on the Day of Pentecost. (Acts 2.1-13)

4 *Dove.* The dove released by Noah after the flood brought back an olive-tree branch as a sign that the waters had receded from the earth (Genesis 8.8-12). After the baptism of Jesus the Holy Spirit came to him in the form of a dove (Matthew 3.16). The dove, the most popular of all symbols for the Holy Spirit, reminds us that God's Spirit is the bringer of peace.

A Why do you think a dove is the most popular symbol for the Holy Spirit? What does the symbol suggest to you?

B Sometimes the Holy Spirit is portrayed in the Bible as a mighty, rushing wind. Which characteristics of the Holy Spirit does this image draw our attention to?

The work of the Holy Spirit

The CCC makes it clear that the Church sees the work of the Holy Spirit running through its whole life and witness. The Church is the place where the Holy Spirit can be experienced. In particular he:

a) inspired the Scriptures, preparing them to be the main source of inspiration for the Church;

b) can be experienced in the Tradition of the Church;

c) inspires the teaching of the magisterium – the teaching ministry of the Church;

d) works through the words and symbols of the liturgy to put people into communion with Christ;

e) intercedes for all believers in prayer;

f) works through the various ministries of the Church, whether they are exercised by the clergy or by the laity;

g) is in the work and witness of the saints through whom he continues his work of salvation.

When Catholics profess their faith in the statement of the Creed – 'I believe in the Holy Spirit' – they are stating their need for God's help in the world today. They receive that help through the inspiration of the Scriptures and the continuing teaching ministry and authority of the Church. Even as they pray and look for inspiration in the lives of those who have lived and died before them, they are recognising that the work of the Holy Spirit is unceasing on their behalf.

ANSWER IN YOUR BOOK …

1 How do Roman Catholics understand the relationship between the different members of the Trinity?

2 What do the different symbols of the Holy Spirit used in the Scriptures teach us about his work.

3 How does the CCC sum up the work of the Holy Spirit?

READ AND DECIDE …

Here are four quotations from the Bible about the Holy Spirit. Read them carefully before answering the questions:

a) "In the beginning God created the heavens and the earth. Now the earth was a formless void, there was darkness over the deep, and God's spirit hovered over the water." (Genesis 1.1,2)
   ❖ This reference comes at the very beginning of the Bible. What do you think it underlines about the Holy Spirit?

b) "This is how Jesus Christ came to be born. His mother Mary was betrothed to Joseph; but before they came to live together she was found to be with child by the Holy Spirit." (Matthew 1.23)
   ❖ What important truth is being emphasised in this reference?

c) "The Spirit too comes to help us in our weakness. For when we cannot choose words in order to pray properly, the Spirit himself expresses our plea in a way that could never be put into words…" (Romans 1.26)
   ❖ What does this verse suggest about prayer and the Holy Spirit?

d) "The love of God has been poured into our hearts by the Holy Spirit which has been given us." (Romans 5.5)
   ❖ What does this verse suggest about the relationship between God the Father and the Holy Spirit?

IN THE GLOSSARY …

Roman Catholic Church; Incarnation; Holy Spirit; Day of Pentecost; Holy Scriptures; New Testament; Baptism; Confirmation; Ordination; Magisterium; Liturgy; Trinity; Sacrament; Creed; Saint; Prophet; Old Testament; Clergy; Laity.

2.11 THE VIRGIN MARY (1)

All of the main Christian Churches accept that Mary was the mother of Jesus. As Martin Luther, the Protestant reformer, states:

> "...the same One who God begot from eternity she herself brought forth in time..."

The Churches, however, diverge over the honour and respect that should be paid to Mary:

1 Whilst giving Mary respect the Protestant Churches do not believe that she was any different to other human beings. She was chosen by God to give birth to Jesus – but no more.

2 The Orthodox Church venerates Mary as they venerate other saints. She is the object of devotion and worship and her painting on icons stimulates this.

3 The Catholic Church gives Mary a central role in their belief and worship. It was through her that the Son of God came into history. Her role as "Mother of God and of the Redeemer..." means that she:

> "...far surpasses all creatures, both in heaven and earth." (The Second Vatican Council)

Mary in the New Testament

Mary is only referred to by name in the Synoptic Gospels and the Acts of the Apostles. In John's Gospel she is called 'the mother of Jesus', or 'his mother' (2.1, 3,5,12; 1.25-26) while the only reference in Paul is 'God sent his Son, born of a woman...' (Galatians 4.4).

In the Synoptic Gospels, Mary is presented as the mother of Jesus Christ. She was engaged to Joseph, a carpenter from Nazareth, when the arch-angel Gabriel appeared to her and told her that she was soon to become the mother of God's Son, the Messiah

A Why do you think that Mary and two other women were the only followers of Jesus found at the cross?

(Matthew 1 and Luke 1 and 2). Mary then travelled to Bethlehem with Joseph and gave birth to the infant Jesus in a stable. The method by which Jesus was conceived in the womb of Mary is called 'the Virgin Birth' and we will look at this closely in the next unit.

When Jesus started to preach, Mary accompanied him to Capernaum and Cana. In Cana she was present at the first miracle that he performed when he turned the water into wine at a wedding-feast (John 2.1-12). She seems to have been on the end of some very sharp words from Jesus on this occasion. Something similar happened later when Mary, and the brothers of Jesus, tried to persuade him to stop preaching (Matthew 12.46-50). Mary then disappeared from the story until we find her present at Calvary when Jesus was crucified (Matthew 27.56).

Mary in the Church today

The CCC draws our attention to certain aspects of 'Mary, Mother of Christ, Mother of the Church.' They are:

a) That from the moment Mary consented to be the mother of God's Son, through to his death and resurrection, she identified herself totally with all that he was doing. That is why, at the end of her life, she was 'taken up, body and soul, into heavenly glory'. This belief, the Assumption of the Blessed Virgin, will be examined more closely in the next unit.

b) Because of her total faithfulness to God, Mary is the 'Church's model of faith and charity'. She is the most superior and 'wholly unique' member of the Church.

c) Mary herself said 'All generations will call me blessed'. The Church rightly honours the Virgin Mary with special devotion. The faithful come to the 'Mother of God' in all their dangers and needs. This devotion is expressed through the special festivals dedicated to the Virgin as well as through prayers directed towards her.

d) The Virgin Mary is a reminder to the Church of its own pilgrimage and journey. At the end of that journey the Church looks forward to being welcomed by the one it venerates as Mother of the Lord in the 'glory of the Most Holy and Undivided Trinity.'

B This is an icon (a religious painting) of the Virgin Mary used by members of the Greek Orthodox faith. Can you find out what members of this Church believe about the Virgin Mary.

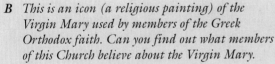

READ AND DECIDE …

On two occasions Jesus spoke very sharply to his mother and the rest of his family. You can read about them for yourself in Matthew 12.46-50 and John 2 1.12. Look at them carefully before answering the following questions:

a) Why did Jesus detach himself from his family on both occasions?

b) Do you think there was some great overriding preoccupation which came between Jesus and his family? If so, what was it?

ANSWER IN YOUR BOOK …

1 What can we learn about the Virgin Mary from the Gospels?

2 How did Mary show herself as willing to subordinate herself to the will of God?

3 How is Mary treated by the Catholic Church today?

FIND OUT AND NOTE …

Carry out some research of your own to find out just what the Roman Catholic Church believes about the Virgin Mary. What was the Annunciation? What is the Virgin Birth? What is the Immaculate Conception? What is the Assumption of the Blessed Virgin?

Keep your notes on these important topics in front of you when you work your way through Unit 2.12.

IN THE GLOSSARY …

Roman Catholic Church; New Testament; Synoptic Gospels; Messiah; Virgin Birth; Assumption of the Blessed Virgin; Rosary; Trinity; Acts of the Apostles; Virgin Mary; Protestant; Orthodox Church; Saint; Icon; Second Vatican Council; St Paul.

2.12 THE VIRGIN MARY (2)

The Catholic Church holds three specific doctrines (beliefs) about the Virgin Mary. It maintains that these beliefs have developed over the centuries under the guidance of the Holy Spirit. Not all of them are found in the Scriptures but, the Church claims, there is nothing in them which is contrary to the teaching of the Bible.

The Virgin Birth

The Nicene Creed makes it clear that the early Church believed that Jesus was 'born of a virgin'. This simply means that Jesus was conceived in the womb of a virgin, Mary, without any human father being involved. Two of the Gospels, Matthew's (1.18-25) and Luke's (1.26-38), explain this by saying that Jesus was conceived by the Holy Spirit. In other words, the conception and birth of Jesus was a divinely-inspired miracle. Strangely, the rest of the New Testament has nothing to say about the Virgin Birth. However, a whole succession of Church Councils from Nicea onwards have all insisted that Jesus was born to a virgin.

From its beginning the Church has used the virgin birth of Jesus to teach that Jesus is perfect, unique and divine. If Jesus had been conceived normally he would have shared humanity's sinful nature. He could not then have saved the world through his death.

The Immaculate Conception

Since the 15th century most Catholics have believed that Mary was free from Original Sin the moment she was conceived in her mother's womb. It did not, however, become part of the official teaching of the Catholic Church until Pope Pius IX was elected Pope.

Soon after his election he consulted with 603 bishops and found that only 56 of them opposed the doctrine. On December 8th, 1854 the doctrine was publicly announced and it became part of the Church's official teaching.

The Assumption of the Virgin Mary

Few Popes were more devoted to the Virgin Mary than Pope Pius XII, who died in 1958. He was particularly devoted to Our Lady of Fatima, who had appeared to

A Why do you think that the Church has insisted that Jesus was born to a virgin?

three small children in the Portuguese town of Fatima in 1917. When he consecrated the whole world to the Immaculate Heart of Mary in 1942, he spoke in Portuguese to emphasise his devotion to Fatima. Then, in 1950, he defined another doctrine of Mary – that of her bodily assumption into heaven.

Catholics share this belief with Orthodox Christians. They believe that Mary's 'crowning glory...was to be preserved from the corruption of the tomb' and to be lifted, body and soul, into heaven. There, Mary reigns as Queen 'at the right hand of her Son, the immortal King of Ages.'

In 1950, ecumenical relations between the Churches were just beginning to get underway. Protestants found another doctrine about the Virgin Mary hard to accept but it went some way towards easing relationships between the Catholic and the Orthodox Churches since this was a belief that Orthodox believers had held for centuries. Both Churches celebrate the feast of the Assumption on August 15th.

ANSWER IN YOUR BOOK ...

1 What is meant by the Virgin Birth?
2 Why has the Church always maintained that the doctrine of the Virgin Birth is important?
3 What is meant by the 'Assumption of the Virgin Mary?'

CAN YOU EXPLAIN?

a) What was the difference between a normal conception and the conception of Jesus?
b) How would you explain what Catholics believe about the Virgin Birth?
c) Does it strike you as strange that, apart from Matthew and Luke, no other writer in the New Testament mentions the Virgin Birth? Can you suggest any reason for this?
d) Do any vitally important Christian beliefs stem from the Virgin Birth of Jesus?

WHAT DO YOU THINK?

Not all Christians believe that Jesus was conceived and born to a virgin.
a) Do you think that this belief is important today?
b) If you think that this belief is still important, what do you think it means to people today?

READ AND DECIDE ...

The CCC draws a parallel between the Virgin Mary and the Catholic Church:

"The Church...by receiving the word of God in faith becomes herself a mother. By preaching and baptism she brings forth sons and daughters who are conceived of the Holy Spirit and are born to God, to a new and immortal life." (64)

Explain, in your own words, the parallel that is drawn here between the Virgin Mary and the Catholic Church.

IN THE GLOSSARY ...

Virgin Mary; Roman Catholic Church; New Testament; Nicene Creed; Gospels; Holy Spirit; Pope; Original Sin; Orthodox Church; Holy Scriptures; Bible; Virgin Birth; Church Council; Immaculate Conception; Assumption of the Blessed Virgin; Protestant.

2.13 SICKNESS AND SUFFERING

Sickness and suffering are among the gravest problems that any believer in God has to face. Illness brings us all face to face with our own powerlessness and limitations. Indeed, as the CCC points out:

> "Every illness can make us glimpse death" (1500)

Suffering and illness can have one of two effects on a person:

a) It can put his or her faith in God under a severe strain. Catholics are not immune to this. Sometimes, it might even compel a person to despair of God and lose their faith altogether.

b) It can help a person towards a greater maturity of faith by showing them what is ultimately important in life and what is not. As the CCC comments:

> "Very often illness provokes a search for God and a return to him." (1501)

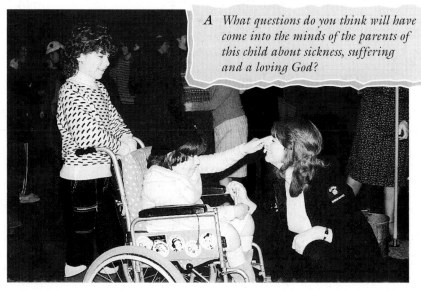

A *What questions do you think will have come into the minds of the parents of this child about sickness, suffering and a loving God?*

Sickness and God

The Old Testament offers us a real insight into the nature of suffering. It was the belief of the Old Testament prophets that sickness was mysteriously linked to sin and evil. Therefore, when a person repented of their sin and returned to God they

B *What aspects of suffering do you find most disturbing?*

experienced the healing of their body as well.

When Christ was seen healing people it was a 'resplendent sign' that God's kingdom had arrived. Jesus offered the people not only healing for their body but also forgiveness for their soul. He alone could do this because he was God's Son. Just as the sick reached out to Jesus to be healed (Refer to READ AND DECIDE...) so the sick today can receive God's healing through the sacraments.

The believer and suffering

The healings of Jesus were not universal. Although they announced the coming of God's kingdom, Jesus did not see this as the most important part of his ministry. That was his death on the cross by which he took the whole weight of the world's sickness and suffering on himself. Christ now invites all believers to share in that by taking up their cross and following him. By doing so they acquire a new outlook on sin and suffering. They begin to share in the same ministry of compassion and service that Jesus himself forged. As we read in Mark 6.12-14:

> "So they set off to preach repentance; and they cast out many devils, and anointed many sick people with oil and cured them."

This is the ministry in which all believers are to share.

The CCC accepts that while some people have a special gift for healing others, even the most intense prayers do not always bring this about. This has always been the case. The CCC reminds Catholics that even St Paul had a mystery affliction ('a thorn in the flesh') which was never taken away. He had to learn that 'my grace is sufficient for you, for my power is made perfect in weakness' (2.Corinthians 12.9) and that the sufferings to be endured can mean:

> "...that in my flesh I complete what is lacking in Christ's afflictions for the sake of his Body, that is, the Church." (Colossians 1.24)

Suffering and healing remain a mystery without any simple answers. The faithful believer has to trust that God is there in the middle of all their pain and distress. In this, they are helped considerably by the Church's sacrament of anointing the sick – see Unit 3.12.

ANSWER IN YOUR BOOK ...

1 What effect can suffering have upon the Christian believer?

2 How was sickness and suffering explained in the Old Testament?

3 What do Catholics believe that Jesus accomplished by his death? How are believers invited to share in this today?

READ AND DECIDE ...

The following references give us a valuable insight into the approach of Jesus towards those who were suffering:

a) Mark 2.5-12

b) Mark 2.17

c) Matthew 25.36

d) Mark 5.34,36

e) Mark 9.23

f) Mark 7.32-36

g) Mark 8.22-25

h) John 9. 6,7

Make your own notes on each of these passages. Then write an essay of about 500 words with the title 'Jesus and suffering'.

USE YOUR IMAGINATION ...

Imagine that you are each of the following people. What kind of questions do you think you would ask? Would any of these situations test your belief in God?

a) The parent of a young baby who has just been diagnosed as having leukaemia.

b) A 13 year old whose parents have just been killed in a car crash.

c) A 40 year old who is left to care for their mother or father as they are dying.

d) A man or a woman who loses a partner after 30 years of married life.

IN THE GLOSSARY ...

Old Testament; Prophet; Sacrament; St Paul.

2.14 DEATH AND BEYOND

There are comparatively few Church documents about death. Most of those that do exist belong to the Middle Ages and reflect the ideas of that period. Not until the Second Vatican Council was there a comprehensive statement of Catholic belief about life after death and the resurrection of the dead. Here we will concern ourselves with the themes of death and judgement. In Unit 2.15 we will look at the teaching of the Church on the destiny of the faithful – the Beatific Vision, Purgatory and the Resurrection of the Body.

Death

For the Christian, the death of Jesus is the model for every human death. It was possible for Jesus to avoid his destiny, but to do this would have destroyed his mission from God. It was only through his death that Jesus could release the Holy Spirit into the world and into the Church. Jesus, therefore, had to accept death just as all believers must accept their death as well.

Death brings to an end our mortal life. It reminds us that all things are passing:

"because man goes to his eternal home…and the dust returns to the earth as it was, and the spirit returns to God who gave it."
(Ecclesiastes 12.5,7)

While we live, body and soul are kept together. At death, they are separated. The body perishes and returns to dust but the soul or spirit lives on. In the Liturgy for the Dead the Church reminds us that:

"…for your faithful, Lord, life is changed, not taken away; and when this earthly dwelling place is destroyed, an eternal home awaits us in heaven."

Judgement

The final judgement of all people is a common theme throughout the Bible and the various Creeds of the Church. Here are two examples:

❖ *The Apostles Creed*. 'He shall come again to judge the living and the dead.'
❖ *The Nicene Creed*. 'He ascended to the heavens and shall come again to judge the living and the dead.'

A *Before we look at the Church's teaching on death and life after death, note down any ideas that you may have about these subjects.*

The time is coming when God the Father will reveal the truth about every person's life – the good that they have done and the evil they have inflicted on others (John 5.28-29). This time of judgement will coincide with the return of Christ to the earth (Matthew 25.13, 31). Whatever sins it has committed, the Church will then be presented to Christ as a pure and spotless 'bride'.

Almost without realising it, we have spoken of two forms of judgement:

a) The general judgement of the world, linked to the Second Coming of Christ.
b) The individual judgement, in which each man and woman will be called to give an account of themselves to God. This takes place at death.

The two forms of judgement are intertwined in the Church's teaching.

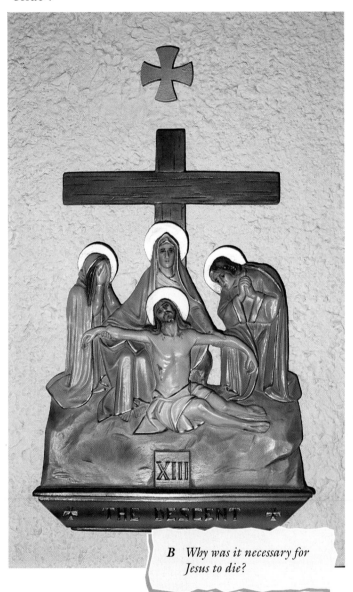

B *Why was it necessary for Jesus to die?*

2.15 LIFE EVERLASTING

Death, for every Christian, is the doorway to everlasting life. This is the prospect which the Catholic Church holds before every dying person who has received the following:

a) The final absolution – by which, assurance is given that all their sins are forgiven.
b) The anointing with oil.
c) The viaticum for the last journey – the final taking of the sacrament of Communion.
d) The final indulgence. (Refer to READ AND DECIDE...).

Death, when it comes, moves as swiftly as the night. It ends all opportunity for a person to work out their own salvation. They must now be judged by the works that they have committed during their lifetime. That judgement will take place in the light of the two chilling questions which Jesus himself asked:

1 "What will a man gain if he wins the whole world and ruins his life?"
2 "What has a man to offer in exchange for his life?"

Each person must answer to Christ since all judgement has been given to him by the Father (Matthew 16.26). From the hands of Christ, each immortal soul must accept the reward, purification or punishment which is considered right.

The reward – heaven

The reward for those who are perfect in love is to see God as he really is. This is the 'Beatific Vision'. Catholics believe that Jesus, by his death, opened heaven to us where there will be:

> "...no more sadness, nor crying, nor pain any more, for the former things have passed away." (Revelation 21.4)

Words cannot express the beauty and happiness found in heaven – called the 'New Jerusalem'. All that we have are 'pictures' – light, life, peace, the heavenly Jerusalem, the wedding banquet, our Father's house, paradise etc. In the words of St Paul:

> "...eye has not seen, nor ear heard, nor has it entered into the heart of man, these things which God has prepared for those who love him." (1.Corinthians 2.9)

The purification – purgatory

Few people are sufficiently pure to enter heaven as soon as they die. For most, a time of purification and cleansing is needed. In the Holy Scriptures (1.Corinthians 3.13), this cleansing is compared to a fire which burns out all impurities from base metal. God alone knows how long a soul will need to spend in purgatory before it is fit to enter heaven.

In the Deuterocanonical book of 2.Maccabees (12.45), Judas Maccabeus is said to have made

A *Why do you think that Catholics believe that there is a place between heaven and hell called purgatory?*

B   This is hell as one artist has pictured it. Do you find it hard to reconcile belief in hell with belief in a God of love?

atonement for the dead. The Church has always taught that making intercession (praying) for the dead may well shorten their stay in purgatory. This not only includes the Mass but also indulgences, penance, almsgiving and prayers. In church, the month of November is set aside to intercede for those in purgatory.

The punishment – hell

For those who reject the love of God and die unrepentant, there is a terrible price to be paid. Anyone who continues to make this free choice through to the time of their death will cut themselves off from fellowship with God after death. The fires of hell do not cleanse, as do the fires of purgatory, but are an everlasting punishment in a place where "...the worm does not die, and the fire is not quenched." (Mark 9.48)

The following points need to be made about hell:

a) God does not wish anyone to go to hell. At every Mass the Church prays that all may be delivered from eternal damnation.

b) Hell is a dramatic warning of the consequences of rejecting God. Jesus frequently spoke of the fires of Gehenna (Hell) – as in Matthew 25.41.

c) The existence of hell should be a great motive for the Church to work for the conversion of the sinner while time remains. (See Matthew 7.13-14)

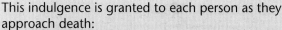

ANSWER IN YOUR BOOK ...

1 How does the Church prepare someone for death?

2 What is the Beatific Vision?

3 What is the link in Catholic belief between heaven and purgatory?

READ AND DECIDE ...

This indulgence is granted to each person as they approach death:

"Go forth, O Christian soul, out of this world, in the name of God the Father Almighty, who created you; in the name of Jesus Christ, the Son of the Living God who suffered for you; in the name of the Holy Spirit, who was poured out upon you; may you take your place today in peace and make your home with God in holy Zion with Mary the Virgin Mother of God, St Joseph and all the angels and saints of God...Return to the Creator who formed you from the dust of the earth, and when your soul leaves your body, may Mary and all the saints come to meet you...May you see your Redeemer face to face."

a) How would you describe the tone of this indulgence? What do you think it is intended to do for the person approaching death?

b) To what extent does the Trinity play an important part in this indulgence?

c) How are the saints intended to comfort the person approaching death?

d) Which phrases are used in this indulgence to refer to heaven? How would you explain them?

IN THE GLOSSARY ...

Absolution; Anointing the sick; Viaticum; Indulgence; Heaven; Purgatory; Hell; Beatific Vision; Mass; Penance; Virgin Mary; Saint; Catholic Church; Sacrament; Soul; St Paul; Holy Scriptures.

3.1 WHAT IS CATHOLICISM?

Catholicism is a rich and diverse religious faith. It is a Christian tradition, a way of life and a community of people all rolled into one. It combines doctrines and beliefs with ways of worshipping and behaving. The Catholic community is a group of people brought together and united in their common history, belief and worship.

What is 'Catholicism'?

The word 'Catholic' comes from two Greek words meaning 'universal' and 'whole'. Usually, it is applied to a member of the Roman Catholic Church but it can also describe the worldwide Christian community itself. Those who share the Catholic faith believe that they share in God's mercy, love and forgiveness through the life, death and resurrection of Jesus of Nazareth.

Early Church leaders used the word to describe the overall Christian community and the individual members of it. In the 4th century St Paciamus, a Spanish bishop said:

> "Christian is my name, Catholic is my surname."

Around the same time St Cyril of Jerusalem spelled out just what the word 'Catholic' means when it is applied to the Church. It has four aspects and means that:

a) The Church is universal – extending throughout the whole world. The community of the followers of Jesus is missionary at heart.
b) The Church teaches universal truths – which have to be accepted by Christian believers everywhere.
c) The Church is the true spiritual home of all people, bringing 'under the sway of true religion all classes of people, rules and subjects, learned and ignorant…'
d) The Church embraces all spiritual virtues and gifts.

From the time of its origin, in the days of the Apostles, through to the present time, the Catholic Church has met each of these conditions. The oldest known 'catechism' of the Church, the Apostles Creed, contains the words:

A Using this African montage as a guide, explain how you think the African church sees itself and its role in society.

"I believe in … the holy catholic church, the communion of saints…"

The Nicene Creed, slightly later but still widely used in Catholic worship, says:

"We believe in one holy, catholic and apostolic Church…"

We will investigate this aspect of the Church much further in Units 3.4 and 3.5.

The Catholic Church strives to be a universal, spiritual family, a religious home for everyone. While it believes that other forms of Christianity are also expressions of God's activity in the world (they were described by the Second Vatican Council as possessing 'degrees of catholicity') it looks upon itself as offering a unique Christian identity. As the recent 'Catechism of the Catholic Church' emphasises, the distinct contribution of the Catholic Church is centred around the following:

❖ The Creed that it believes.
❖ The seven sacraments that it celebrates.
❖ The acceptance of 'apostolic succession', leading to the supreme authority of the Pope.
❖ The unique importance of the Virgin Mary in worship.

You will find out much more about each of these in the course of this book.

B   What work do you think the Catholic Church should be doing in the U.K?

ANSWER IN YOUR BOOK …

1 What does the word 'catholic' mean?

2 How did St Cyril of Jerusalem explain the word 'catholic'?

3 Which phrases about the 'catholicity' of the Church are used in the Apostles and Nicene Creeds?

CAN YOU EXPLAIN?

a) Can you explain the difference between 'Catholic' and 'catholic'?

b) Can you explain just what the word 'catholic' means in relation to the Church?

c) Can you explain what the Second Vatican Council might have meant when it talked about 'degrees of catholicity' in relation to other branches of the Christian Church?

d) Can you explain what the Creeds might mean when they call the Church 'holy', 'apostolic' and 'catholic'?

WHAT DO YOU THINK?

We will have more to say about Church unity throughout the book. At this stage, though, just do a little preliminary thinking:

a) Why do you think that the ideal situation would be to have one Christian Church?

b) What do you think are the main obstacles standing in the way of Church unity?

c) Do you think that the Church should make every effort possible in the future to become "one"?

IN THE GLOSSARY …

Catholic Church; Second Vatican Council; Creed; Sacrament; Pope; Virgin Mary; Apostle; Apostolic Succession.

3.2 WHAT IS DISTINCTIVE ABOUT THE CATHOLIC CHURCH?

There are, of course, many different branches (or denominations) of the Christian Church. With 1,500,000 members worldwide, however, the Catholic Church is by far the largest of these. Roman Catholicism has its own very clear identity and can be distinguished from the other Churches in three main ways. By looking at these we get to the heart and soul of what being a Catholic is all about:

a) The Catholic Church has an intense commitment to the sacraments. Back in the 5th century, Augustine provided us with the most well-known definition of a 'Sacrament':

> "… the visible form of an invisible grace'.

Opening the second session of the Second Vatican Council in 1963, Pope Paul VI defined a sacrament as:

> "… a reality imbued with the hidden presence of God'.

Put it another way: Catholicism is a faith which sees the divine in the human; the unknown in the known and the infinite in the finite. To the Catholic Faith everything is sacred. A sacrament is a visible form in which the blessing of God comes to each person. As we shall discover in Unit 4, the Catholic Church recognises seven such sacraments although most Protestant Churches only accept two – baptism and Holy Communion.

b) Linked with the importance of the sacraments is another essential principle of the Catholic Church – that of mediation. Because we are naturally sinful, we cannot experience God directly. Any experience that we have of God must come to us through other human beings, or elements taken from the world of human experience. This is where the priest performs a vital role. He is much more important in the Catholic tradition than in any other Church. His work is to focus the presence of God for the benefit of both individual believers and the whole Catholic community. This especially happens when the priest celebrates the Mass on behalf of the whole congregation. The principle of mediation, however, goes much wider than this. It explains the emphasis in the Catholic Faith on the Virgin Mary, the mother of Jesus. The Gospels show her as being especially close to her son. Now, Catholics believe, she is uniquely placed in heaven to pray to God for all believers on earth.

A These elements, which you will recognise, are used in the sacrament of Holy Communion (the Mass). They pass on God's blessing to members of the congregation. Can you think of any different elements which are used in the other sacraments for the same purpose?

c) Linked with both sacramentality and mediation is the 'community' aspect of the Catholic faith. As important as an individual's relationship with God is, it must always be understood in a Church situation. For instance, the sacraments are essential for a person's growth in the Christian life yet these can only be celebrated and experienced within the Church.

B *What does it mean to speak of the priest as being the mediator between God and human beings?*

3.3 THE CHURCH – ORGANISATION AND BELIEF

There were many rituals in the early Christian Church which became essential parts of worship. Two of these soon emerged as being particularly important:

1 Baptism (an adult ritual cleansing using water) was required for conversion to Christianity, just as it had been to Judaism. From the beginning it was used as a way of participating in the death and resurrection of Jesus as well as enjoying the forgiveness of God. The practice of baptising infants did not begin until several centuries later.

A *What was the link between the original disciples of Jesus and later bishops?*

2 The command of Jesus to repeat his last meal with his disciples transformed an ordinary meal of fellowship into a sacred ritual called the Eucharist ('thanksgiving'). When Christians began to meet on Sundays instead of the Jewish Sabbath Day the Eucharist became part of the regular celebration of the resurrection of Jesus. This meal was soon recognised as a re-creation of the sacrifice of Christ and this is how the Catholic Church sees it today.

Organising the young Church

Catholic tradition maintains that the Church was organised by Jesus when he appointed the twelve Apostles and gave them authority to lead the Church after his death. Soon prophets, teachers, healers, helpers and those who spoke in tongues (1.Corinthians 12.28) emerged as leaders. By the end of the 1st century the Church had developed into a reasonably complex organisation.

Soon after the death and resurrection of Jesus the early Apostles had become travelling missionaries – an 'apostle' being someone who was sent. They seem to have appointed 'bishops' or 'deacons' to run the churches in their absence. After the deaths of the original Apostles the bishops emerged as those responsible for public worship and, by the end of the 1st century, they alone had the authority to conduct the Eucharist.

In the 2nd century there were many challenges to the traditional beliefs of the Church. In response, the Church began to set down its own orthodox beliefs for the first time. Irenaeus, an important Christian leader, set down his own 'Rule of Faith'. It included belief in the following:

a) One God, the Father and Creator of all things.
b) The incarnation, the birth of God in Jesus.
c) The Holy Spirit, the prophetic power behind those who foretold the coming of Jesus.

Ignatius of Antioch (died 107 CE) was the first leader to speak of the 'Catholic Church'. He encouraged the position of the bishop as the supreme church leader, one who mirrored God's authority over all things. Sometime around 165 CE the first meeting, or synod, of bishops took place as Rome began to emerge as the main centre of Christianity. Special authority was given to the Bishop of Rome, who later came to be called the Pope. (see Units 3.8 and 3.9)

In the 4th century the Emperor Constantine made Sunday the official day of rest in the Empire and December 25th, the feast of the birthday of the Roman sun god, the day for celebrating the birth of Jesus. Constantine also encouraged Catholic Christianity with many pagans being converted. Many pagan customs also became part of the Catholic liturgy. These included devotion to relics, the kiss as a sign of devotion, the practice of kneeling and the use of candles and incense. The clergy of the Catholic Church were officially recognised by the Empire and the priesthood became a full-time occupation. The Council of Nicea, ordered by Constantine, was a watershed in the Church's history.

B *Constantine, the first Roman Emperor converted to Christianity. Find out all that you can about Constantine and the impact that he had upon the Christian Church.*

ANSWER IN YOUR BOOK ...

1 What change took place when Christians began to meet on Sunday instead of the Jewish Sabbath Day?

2 What were the three basic beliefs outlined by Ignatius?

3 How was Catholic Christianity affected by pagan beliefs in the time of Constantine?

CAN YOU EXPLAIN?

a) Why was baptism an important symbol in the early Christian Church?

b) How did the Eucharist develop out of a simple fellowship meal?

c) How did the early Church develop a multi-faceted ministry? Why did this happen?

d) How did Rome emerge as the main centre of Christianity?

IN YOUR OWN WORDS ...

In your own words, define each of the following in two or three sentences:

a) Baptism

b) The Eucharist

c) Sunday

d) The Sabbath Day

e) Apostle

f) Prophet

g) Relic

IN THE GLOSSARY ...

Baptism; Eucharist; Sunday; Sabbath Day; Apostle; Prophet; Speaking in tongues; Bishop; Bishop of Rome; Pope; Relic; Disciple; Catholic Church; Deacon; Incarnation; Holy Spirit; Priesthood.

3.4 THE ONE, HOLY CHURCH

There are two aspects to the Christian Church:

1 The Church is worldwide ('catholic' or 'universal') and all Christians, of whatever denomination, are a part of it. The word 'church' in Greek, ekklesia, means 'called out' and refers to the fact that the Church is different from the rest of society. Christians are those people called by God to belong to a distinctive community. This is the Church which the Creed describes as being:

> "...one holy, catholic and apostolic Church..."

More about this aspect of the Church in Unit 3.5.

2 The Church is broken down into different denominations or branches. Most of the major denominations are universal but it is also through them that the Church takes on a local form – the Roman Catholics, the Church of England, the Orthodox Church, the Salvation Army, the Methodists, the Baptists, the Quakers etc. Each of these Churches has its own way of worshipping and organising itself. At local, if not at international level, the different Churches are finding ways to work and worship together.

The characteristics of the Church

Within the New Testament two very important 'images' of the Church emerge: the Church as the 'people of God' and the Church as the 'body of Christ'. These powerful images illuminate our understanding of the Church as a whole. We will look at both of them in detail in Unit 3.6. Here we concentrate our attention on three distinctive characteristics of the Christian Church:

a) *The Church as a mystery.* For centuries the Church has been called the 'mystical body of Christ'. In a letter written by Pope Pius XII in 1943, he commented that there could be no more fitting title for the Church. It highlights the Catholic belief that however the Church is explained in human terms it remains, at heart, a mystery. Founded by Jesus Christ to carry out the Father's plan of salvation the Church is, in the words of Paul, 'a great mystery' (Eph 5.32). In fact, the Church is a sacrament since it is the visible sign of the presence of God in the world. Talking of the Church as a sacrament reminds us that the word 'mystical' was first applied to the sacrament of the Eucharist. There is an

A What do you think that Paul meant when he described the Christian Church as a 'great mystery'?

B   The Pope meeting with the Archbishop of Canterbury, the head of the Church of England. What kind of things do you think prevent a closer cooperation, or even unity, between the different Churches?

obvious link between the body of Christ shared in the Eucharist and the body of Christ which is the Church.

b) *The Church is one.* Although it takes many forms the Christian Church is essentially one. The Catholic Church offers itself to all other Churches under the headship of the Pope, as the focus of that unity. It is a unity which stems from the oneness of the Trinity and is guaranteed by the work of the Holy Spirit. Externally it is shown by:

❖ the profession of the one faith received directly from the Apostles;
❖ the celebration of a single worship (especially the sacraments);
❖ The line of bishops appointed by apostolic succession.

This is why the bishops at the Second Vatican Council insisted that the 'one true Church' subsists in the Catholic Church, which is governed by the successors of Peter and the bishops who are in communion with him.

c) *The Church is holy.* The Church is 'the holy people of God' and its members are 'saints'. Through belonging to the Church, people are made holy. The saints and especially the Virgin Mary intercede on behalf of those struggling with the faith.

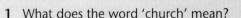

ANSWER IN YOUR BOOK ...

1   What does the word 'church' mean?
2   Which are the two aspects of the Church?
3   What is the relationship between the one Church and the different Churches?

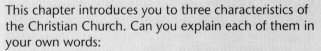

IN YOUR OWN WORDS ...

This chapter introduces you to three characteristics of the Christian Church. Can you explain each of them in your own words:

a) The Church as the 'mystical body of Christ'.
b) The Church as one.
c) The Church as holy.

READ AND DECIDE ...

A quote from the opening of the Second Vatican Council's document 'Dogmatic Constitution of the Church':

"Christ is the light of humanity; and it is, accordingly, the heart-felt desire of this sacred Council being gathered together in the Holy Spirit, that, by proclaiming his Gospel to every creature, it may bring all men that light of Christ which shines out visibly from the Church."

a) What do you think the phrase 'Christ is the light of humanity' means?
b) Why do you think the Second Vatican Council was called a 'sacred Council'?
c) Who drew the various members of the Council together?
d) Where is the 'light of Christ' most noticeably seen?

IN THE GLOSSARY ...

Church; Denomination; Creed; New Testament; St Paul; Sacrament; Eucharist; Catholic Church; Pope; Trinity; Holy Spirit; Apostle; Bishop; Apostolic Succession; Second Vatican Council; St Peter; Saint; Virgin Mary.

3.5 THE CATHOLIC, APOSTOLIC CHURCH

The Catholic Church believes that it has a God-given mission to the world. It claims to be the bridge between the life of God on earth and in eternity. Two claims which it makes for itself , in particular, mark out the Catholic Church as a unique and divine creation. These two claims are:

1 *That the Church is 'catholic'.* Notice that this is 'catholic' with a small 'c'. The CCC explains that the word 'catholic' used in this sense means 'universal, according to the whole, totality'. Christ is to be found everywhere in the Church since he is the head of the Church. The Catholic Church is the true Church because:

* It has the orthodox, and correct, profession of faith. This profession goes all the way back to the origins of the Church.
* It has the full complement of sacraments and uses them to deepen the faith of its members. This it shares with the Orthodox Church, the closest of all the other Churches to the Catholic Church in belief and worship.
* It has a ministry (Pope, cardinals, bishops and clergy) which is in a direct line of succession from the original Apostles. The authority of this ministry comes from the Apostles themselves, who derived their authority directly from Jesus.

The Catholic Church was born on the Day of Pentecost and will remain the true Church until the Second Coming of Christ.

2 *That the Church is 'apostolic'.* The CCC underlines the link between the original Apostles and the Catholic Church today in three distinct ways:
* The Apostles were chosen to be witnesses to Christ during his earthly life and the Catholic Church has built itself on the foundation which they laid down.
* Through the power of the Holy Spirit the testimony and teaching of the Apostles has been handed down through the Church from generation to generation. The Catholic Church has faithfully guarded and passed on that tradition.
* The leaders of the Catholic Church (from the Pope downwards) are all successors to the Apostles. Through them the testimony of the Apostles is jealously guarded.

A The Divine Liturgy is taking place in an Orthodox Church. Can you find out why the Orthodox Church separated from the Catholic Church in the Great Schism of 1054?

Members of the true Church

Who belongs to the 'true Church'?

a) Those who accept all the means of salvation and are in communion with the Catholic Church.

b) Those who accept the means of salvation (the sacraments) but do not accept the Pope's authority. This applies to the Orthodox Churches.

c) Those who are united with the Catholic Church in baptism but do not accept the other sacraments. This includes all Protestants who are referred to as 'separated brethren'.

d) Those who are not Christian, and pride of place here belongs to the Jews. Also included are the followers of Islam who worship one God and accept the faith of Abraham. Finally, there are those who seek after God but who, as yet, have not found him.

To all these people the Catholic Church is called upon to be a beacon. This is the work of 'evangelisation' to which the Church is fully committed. According to the CCC the Church is that boat which

"… in full sail of the Lord's cross, by the breath of the Holy Spirit, navigates safely in this world."

B *This Communion Service is taking place in an Anglican Church. What do you think the Second Vatican Council meant when it referred to members of this Church as 'separated brethren'?*

This Church is extremely important. As we discovered in Unit 2.15, the belief that the Pope is 'infallible' is a central Catholic doctrine. Less known, however, is the Catholic belief that the whole people of God (the Church) has an infallible understanding of God's truth. It has the full message of Christ inspired by the Holy Spirit and so cannot falter in matters of faith and belief. This doctrine is called the 'Sensus Fidelium' (the Understanding of the Faithful).

ANSWER IN YOUR BOOK …

1 What does the word 'catholic' mean?

2 What is the attitude of the Catholic Church towards Christians of other denominations and towards members of other religious faiths?

3 What is the 'Sensus Fidelium'?

CAN YOU EXPLAIN?

a) Can you explain why the Catholic Church believes itself to be the true Church?

b) Can you explain the link between the original Apostles and the Catholic Church?

c) Can you explain how the Church has attempted to safeguard the tradition handed down by the Apostles?

d) Can you explain the meaning of the word 'evangelisation'?

WHAT DO YOU THINK?

The First Vatican Council was convened in 1869. It said this about the Church:

"Hence it is that the Church that really is catholic, must at the same time be marked out by the prerogatives of unity, holiness and apostolic succession."

a) What are the four true marks of the genuine Church?

b) Why do you think that these particular characteristics are thought to be so important?

c) What is meant by 'apostolic succession'?

IN THE GLOSSARY …

Orthodox Church; Anglican Church; Protestant; Creed; New Testament; Sacrament; Holy Spirit; Apostle; Bishop; Virgin Mary; Pope; Catholic Church; Cardinal; Clergy; Day of Pentecost; Second Coming of Christ; Sensus Fidelium.

3.6 PICTURES OF THE CHURCH

There are two pictures, or images, of the Church which figure prominently in the New Testament. From them we can gain an insight into how the early Christians understood the Church.

The Church as the People of God

The Old Testament tells us that the Jews were chosen by God to be a special nation. God entered into an agreement (a covenant) with them through which he revealed himself to the Jewish people in three ways:

a) He delivered the Jewish people from over 400 years of Egyptian slavery – an event known as the Exodus. Jews continue to celebrate this deliverance each year in their festival of Passover.

b) He gave to the Israelites (Jews) their unique laws (called the Torah – Teaching) on Mount Sinai, including the Ten Commandments.

c) He made it possible for the Jews both to conquer and enter their Promised Land (Canaan). By this time the Jews had come to believe strongly in the one God who controlled history.

In the centuries that followed the Jews were to suffer at the hands of many different enemies. God promised them a leader, the Messiah, who would lead them all into truth but when that figure came they rejected him. His name was Jesus. God has never rejected the Jews. They remain a very important part of God's future plans for humanity.

The New Testament, however, indicates that the Church, rather than the Jews, are now the 'people of God' and 'the chosen race'. These two words, 'people' and 'race', emphasise the unity of all those people who belong to the Church. The Church is made up of all those individuals who share, through baptism, a common belief in God and a common faith.

There is more. The terms also emphasise the 'family' aspect of the Church. Through baptism, all Catholics have become members of the family of God. Not only are they 'sons and daughters' of God but also 'brothers and sisters' of Christ. They are united by the love of God which has been spread in their hearts by the Holy Spirit.

The Church as the Body of Christ

St Paul speaks of the Church as the 'body of Christ'. This conjures up a picture of the Church being similar to a human body with Christ himself as the head. The image emphasises two aspects of the Catholic Church:

A Baptism is an important symbol in the Catholic Church. What use does the Church makes of this particular sacrament? What does it symbolise?

1 Just as the human body is made up of many parts so too are there many different parts to the Catholic Church. Continuing the analogy, every part must play its role if the human body is to function properly. Likewise, within the Church every part is dependent on all the others. As St Paul stressed, the unity of the Church is much more important than the welfare of each individual member:

> "There is one Body, one Spirit, just as you were all called into one and the same hope when you were called. There is one Lord, one faith, one baptism and one God who is Father of all, over all, through all and within all." (Ephesians 4.4-6)

2 The closeness of the head and the body underlines the closeness between the Church (the body) and Christ (the head). The head fulfils an essential function for the well-being of the body as a whole. It provides the sense of direction as well as being the basis of the body's unity and strength. In the same way, Christ is the head of the Church and is that body's source of strength and direction.

Within the Church there are many sources of unity:

a) Its single allegiance to God through Jesus Christ.
b) The inspiration which it receives from the Holy Spirit.
c) The one faith which all Christians share with one another.
d) The one baptism which opens the door to membership of the one Church.
e) The one God 'who is Father of all, over all, through all and within all.'

B *Who, according to the New Testament, make up the Church of Christ?*

ANSWER IN YOUR BOOK ...

1 What does it mean to speak of the Jews as being the 'chosen people of God'?

2 How has the Church now become 'the people of God'?

3 What does it mean to speak of the Church as being 'the body of Christ'?

WHAT DO YOU THINK?

Here are two quotations from the Bible which have strong links with each other.

❖ "...you know that now, if you obey my voice and hold fast to my covenant, you of all nations shall be my very own for all the earth is mine. I will count you a kingdom of priests, a consecrated nation." (Exodus 19.5,6)

❖ "You are a chosen race, a royal priesthood, a consecrated nation, a people set apart to sing the praises of God who called you out of the darkness into his wonderful light." (1.Peter 2.9)

a) What do you think it means to speak of Israel as being 'God's Chosen People'?

b) What do you think it means to call the Church a 'chosen race...a people set apart'?

c) What do you think Peter means when he speaks here of 'darkness' and 'light'?

d) What do the terms 'darkness' and 'light' mean when they are applied to the Church and its mission?

IN THE GLOSSARY ...

Church; New Testament; St Paul; Holy Spirit; Baptism; Old Testament; Exodus; Passover; Torah; Ten Commandments; Messiah; Catholic Church.

3.7 THE COMMUNION OF SAINTS

After confessing its belief in the 'Holy, Catholic Church' the Apostles Creed adds:

> "...and the communion of saints."

This particular phrase refers to a very important belief of Roman Catholics. It can be understood in two different ways:

1 *As a 'communion in holy things'*. This was the earliest way in which the phrase was understood. We are told in Acts 2.42 that the earliest Christian community:

> "...remained faithful to the teaching of the apostles, to the brotherhood, to the breaking of bread and to prayers."

From this the CCC points out the basic meaning of the phrase 'the communion of saints'. It is a communion in the following:

a) The Faith. The Faith is a treasure of the greatest possible value which has been passed on to the Church from the Apostles. The Church now has the responsibility of making sure that the Faith is passed down in its purest form.

b) The Sacraments. The Sacraments are God's sacred gift to the Church, linking each believer with God. This gift is to be shared with all true believers.

c) The charisms (gifts of the Holy Spirit). Within the Church the Holy Spirit distributes his gifts for the strengthening and deepening of the fellowship. Each member of the Church shares in these gifts. Should any member of the Church be needy then their needs can be met. As the 'Sanctorum Communio' states:

> "None of us lives to himself, and none of us dies to himself."

2 *As the 'communion of the Church of heaven and earth'*. Above everything else the Church is a fellowship. It is a fellowship called into being by the Father, in Christ, through the power of the Holy Spirit (Hebrews 2.14-17; John 1.14 and 2.Corinthians 13.13). The important thing is that this fellowship is not broken by death – an emphasis which is also clearly found in the Orthodox Church. The 'communion of saints' links together all those who are faithful in this life with those who have

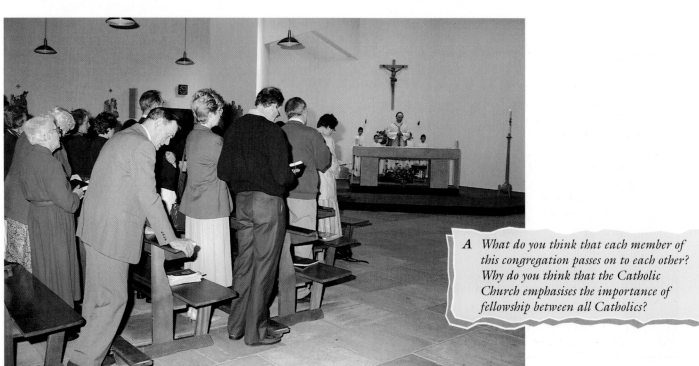

A What do you think that each member of this congregation passes on to each other? Why do you think that the Catholic Church emphasises the importance of fellowship between all Catholics?

entered the life beyond. The CCC spells this idea out more clearly. It says that there are three stages to the Church:

a) There are those who are, at the present time, 'pilgrims on earth'. Our pilgrimage is hard and we need all the help we can get from those who have gone ahead of us.

b) There are those who 'have died and are being purified'. This refers to those people who are currently in purgatory. This intermediate place of purification is discussed further in Units 2.14 and 2.15.

c) There are those who are 'in glory, contemplating in full light, God himself triune and one, exactly as he is…' In other words, there are those among the 'communion of saints' who have passed from purgatory to heaven.

B *What do Roman Catholics believe to be the link between these worshippers praying and those who have gone before them into the next life?*

What are the consequences of this? Those who have reached heaven continually pray (intercede) for those in purgatory and those still on earth. As far as the Church is concerned they:

> "…establish the whole Church more firmly in holiness, lend nobility to the worship which the Church offers on earth to God, and in many ways contribute to its great upbuilding."

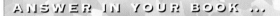

ANSWER IN YOUR BOOK …

1 What does it mean to speak of the 'communion of saints' as a 'communion in holy things'?

2 How does the 'communion of saints' bring together those who are alive and those who have died?

3 What are the three stages of the Church?

TO THINK ABOUT …

St Thomas Aquinas is recognised as the most important Church Father. He lived in the 13th century and his teaching has had an enormous influence on the Catholic Church ever since. He wrote:

> "Since all the faithful form one body, the good of each is communicated to the others….We must therefore believe that there exists a communion of goods in the Church. But the most important member is Christ, since he is the head…Therefore, the riches of Christ are communicated to all the members, through the sacraments…"

There are two important things here for you to think about and discuss:

a) How does each member of the Church communicate their 'good' to each other in practice? What do you think the 'good' refers to?

b) How do the sacraments share the 'riches' of Christ with all those who participate? What do you think these 'riches' are?

READ AND DECIDE …

In his 'Credo of the People of God' Pope Paul VI said:
> "We believe in the communion of all the faithful in Christ, of those who are pilgrims on the earth, of the dead who have achieved their purification, of the blessed in heaven, who together form one Church, and we believe that in this communion the merciful love of God and of his saints will always hear our prayers."

a) How is the 'communion of saints' made up?

b) What practical difference might the 'communion of saints' make to people still living?

IN THE GLOSSARY …

Apostles Creed; Roman Catholic Church; Sacrament; Holy Spirit; Purgatory; Heaven; Orthodox Church.

When the Roman Empire collapsed in 410 the Catholic Church provided valuable leadership. By this time the Church had become responsible for looking after the poor, the oppressed and the old. The bishops and the clergy were expected to provide much-needed practical as well as spiritual help. They also had considerable political influence. On two occasions, for instance, Pope Leo I (440-461) negotiated with the Vandals to prevent them attacking the city of Rome.

Pope Leo I

Pope Leo I was one of the strongest of all Popes. He emphasised that Christ had built his Church on Peter, the Rock, and so all respect should be given to the Bishop of Rome, the Pope. His decrees should carry greater authority than any coming from the Bishops of Alexandria, Antioch, Jerusalem or Constantinople. Many problems within the Church pointed to the need for strong leadership and this, Pope Leo declared, could only come from Rome. He tried to consolidate this power in 451 at the Council of Chalcedon when he asked that a 'Tome' he had written should be accepted as if it had come from St Peter himself. His wish was finally granted although the matter was the subject of intense debate.

Later Popes

Pope Gregory the Great (590-604), like Leo before him, had great political power. He also strengthened his power within the Church and used it to good purpose. He took care of the poor and needy and asked the monks in the Benedictine order to spread the Gospel. Augustine was dispatched, along with many

A Why do you think that Pope Leo I was anxious to make the papacy as powerful as possible?

monks, to evangelise England. Under Pope Gregory II (715-31) the Pope joined the monks in opposing the political authorities. The conflict was over the use of images and icons in religious worship, which the political authorities opposed.

Under Charlemagne the political and religious authorities were brought together. At a Christmas Mass in 800 CE the old Roman Empire was almost reconstituted by Charlemagne and the power of the Pope as the agent of God was re-affirmed. The Holy Roman Empire was now born. After Charlemagne's death, however, many Popes insisted that they had the right to interfere in political matters. In response, a whole succession of Emperors appointed their own Popes, bishops and clergy, giving themselves effective control over the Church.

Ironically, the effect of this on the Church was not altogether bad. When Henry III was king, for instance, he wanted the Church to give a strong moral and spiritual lead to the people and so only appointed holy bishops and popes. Pope Gregory VII (1073-85), the greatest Pope since Gregory I, insisted that the Church must be free to appoint its own leaders. In particular, he:

❖ issued decrees against the marrying of the clergy;
❖ declared the offpring of the clergy to be illegitimate;
❖ issued decrees against simony (buying or selling promotion within the church order) and church leaders being chosen by non-Church authorities. He also issued a famous statement, 'Dictatus papae', giving the Pope absolute power.

B   Why do you think that Pope Gregory III insisted that the Church should be free to appoint its own leaders?

a) Can you find out what brought about the final collapse of the Roman Empire in 410?

b) Can you find out what happened when Augustine reached the shores of Britain with his fellow-monks carrying the Christian Gospel?

c) Can you find out some more about each of the following:
   ❖ Pope Leo I
   ❖ Pope Gregory the Great (Pope Gregory VII)
   ❖ Augustine
   ❖ Charlemagne

d) What can you find out about the Church punishment of excommunication? Why was it the most serious punishment that the Church could impose?

e) Can you find out about one occasion in Britain's history when there was a clash between the power of the Church and the power of the State? Who emerged victorious on that particular occasion? Do you think there is a real danger of the Church becoming too involved in political affairs? If so, what do you think that danger is?

Inevitably, there was a clash between the religious and secular authorities. King Henry IV declared that Gregory was not a genuine Pope and Gregory responded by excommunicating Henry. The King deposed Gregory, who died with the people turned against him.

WRITE AN ESSAY ...

Describe, in about 500 words, 'The Rise of the Papacy'.

ANSWER IN YOUR BOOK ...

1   Describe the constant conflict in the early Church between those with political power and those with spiritual power.

2   Why do you think that political leaders were unhappy about the use of icons and statues in the Catholic Church?

3   How important do you think that the victory of Pope Leo I at the Council of Chalcedon over the power of the Pope turned out to be?

IN THE GLOSSARY ...

St Peter; Monk; Bishop of Rome; Pope; Benedictines; Catholic Church; Bishop; Clergy; Gospel; Icon; Excommunication.

3.9 THE POPE

One of the most important distinguishing marks of the Catholic faith is the importance which it attaches to the Papacy. In the eyes of many it is this, rather than anything else, which marks out Catholicism from the other Christian traditions. This is why the issue has always been a divisive one in the Christian Church. It was largely responsible for the Great Schism (the split between the Catholic and Orthodox Churches) in the 11th century and the Reformation (the split between the Catholic Church and the Protestants) in the 16th Century.

There are two central beliefs about the Pope which are held by Roman Catholics:

a) *The primacy of the Pope.* The Pope is the Bishop of Rome – a title which was first held by St Peter. He is also the Bishop of the whole Church and so not only exercises authority over the whole Catholic Church but also claims to have supreme authority over the whole Christian Church.

b) *The gift of infallibility.* This belongs to the Pope when he solemnly speaks 'ex cathedra' (from the throne) as the earthly head of the Church on issues of faith, belief and moral behaviour. The Pope only does this occasionally when he promulgates (declares) a new doctrine or belief for the Church.

Peter in the New Testament

The Pope's power in the Catholic Church stems from Peter's in the Gospels. As the most prominent disciple of Jesus, according to the New Testament he was:

1 the first to be called, along with his brother (Andrew), to be a disciple – Mark 1.16-18;
2 listed first among the Twelve – Mark 3.16-19;
3 frequently the spokesman for the disciples – Matthew 18.21;
4 renamed by Jesus as 'the rock' and given the keys to heaven – Matthew 16.18;
5 the first apostolic witness to the resurrection of Jesus from the dead – Luke 24.12;
6 prominent in the early Church, preaching the first Christian sermon on the Day of Pentecost – Acts 2.

We cannot, however, be sure how Peter met his death. The strong belief is that he went to Rome and was killed by the mad Roman Emperor, Nero, sometime between 62 and 64 CE.

A Find out all that you can about Pope John Paul II.

The Second Vatican Council and the Papacy

For centuries the Pope had exercised autocratic power within the Church and the Second Vatican Council tried to change this. While recognising that the Pope still had 'full, supreme and universal power over the Church', the bishops were no longer thought of as the Pope's vicars or delegates. Their authority comes from Christ, not from the Pope, and they have 'a mission to teach all nations and preach the gospel to every creature'. They do not govern their dioceses 'as vicars of the Roman pontiff' and they have a considerable amount of freedom to make their own decisions. The bishops and the Pope are called to work together. In particular they should:

a) work in and through the local church;
b) faithfully preach the Gospel;
c) administer the sacraments;
d) serve their flock (the people for whom they are responsible) with love.

B Find out all that you can about St Peter and his importance to the Catholic Church.

ANSWER IN YOUR BOOK ...

1 What do Roman Catholics believe about the Pope?

2 Why is St Peter an important figure in Roman Catholic belief?

3 What contribution did the Second Vatican Council make towards understanding the place of the Pope in the Roman Catholic Church?

READ AND DECIDE ...

We read these words in Matthew 16.13-20:

"When Jesus came to the region of Caesarea Philippi he put this question to his disciples, 'Who do the people say the Son of Man is?' And they said, 'Some say he is John the Baptist, some Elijah and others Jeremiah or one of the prophets.' 'But you', he said, 'who do you say I am?' Then Simon Peter spoke up, 'You are the Christ', he said, 'the Son of the Living God.' Jesus replied, 'Simon, son of Jonah, you are a happy man! Because it was not flesh and blood that revealed this to you but my Father in heaven. So now I say to you: You are Peter and on this rock I will build my Church. And the gates of the underworld can never hold out against it. I will give you the keys of the kingdom of heaven... Whatever you bind on earth shall be considered bound in heaven. Whatever you loose on earth shall be considered loosed in heaven."

a) Why do you think that Jesus told Peter that it could only have been God who revealed to him his true identity?

b) There is a play on words here over the name of Peter. Can you find out what it is?

c) Why do Roman Catholics, on the basis of this passage, believe that the Church is built on Peter?

d) How has the Church understood the words 'I will give you the keys of the kingdom of heaven...'?

e) Look up Matthew 16.19. What authority does this seem to give to the successor of St Peter?

IN THE GLOSSARY ...

Pope; Roman Catholic Church; Great Schism; Reformation; Bishop of Rome; St Peter; Ex Cathedra; Gospels; Second Vatican Council; Bishop; Sacrament; New Testament; Protestant; Diocese; Disciple; Day of Pentecost; Gospel.

3.10 RELIGIOUS ORDERS

The monastic movement really began in the 4th century when men and women began to make their way into the desert to dedicate themselves to God. They saw themselves as following the example of Jesus, who spent 40 days in the desert after he had been baptised by John the Baptist (Mark 1.12,13). There were two reasons why the desert was believed to be a spiritually important location:

a) It allowed people to practise a life of self-denial without any material comforts.

b) It was believed to be the home of evil spirits and so was the scene for many conflicts between the powers of good and evil.

In the beginning they were hermits rather than monks but, before long, they began to form themselves into religious communities.

A *Find out all that you can about St Benedict and the order which he established.*

The Benedictines

St Benedict (480-547) is generally held to be the founder of the monastic movement such as we know it. He formed the Benedictine order of monks and nuns at Monte Cassino, in Italy, and became its first abbot. Known as the 'Black Monks' because of the colour of their habits, or clothing, they lived according to the 'Rule of St Benedict'. This Rule emphasises the following:

1 Stability. Monks normally stay in the same monastery from the time they take their vows until they die.
2 The importance of study.
3 A balance between community prayer, work and relaxation.
4 Total obedience to the Abbot, who is elected by the monks themselves.
5 Living a life of poverty.
6 Living a life of chastity.

The later movement

By the 12th century there were some 2000 religious houses following a life based on poverty, chastity and obedience. By the end of the 13th century three important monastic orders had been established:

a) *The Cistercians.* This order, founded in 1098 at Citeaux, believed that the Benedictines had become too worldly. Bernard of Clairveaux rebuked Popes and Emperors alike for their life-styles. He gave to the Church an emphasis on the following:
   ❖ the Virgin Mary;
   ❖ private prayer and meditation;
   ❖ private rather than public confession and penitence.

b) *The Franciscans.* In Italy a nobleman, Francis of Assissi, inspired many disciples when he decided to imitate the simple lifestyle of Jesus. He gave up all his possessions and travelled from town to town preaching a message of repentance, trust and respect for the whole of creation. After spending much time begging, the Order later turned to the Catholic

Church for support.
Around the same time, a
similar Order of nuns was
formed called the Order of
Poor Clares which followed
the same principles as the
Franciscans.

c) *The Dominicans.* Founded
in 1216, the purpose of the
Dominicans from the
beginning was to teach. As
a community the
Dominicans broke with the
tradition of appointing an
abbot for his life-time and
elected its own Superiors for
a limited time.

Other religious Orders also
developed. The Carmelites and
the Augustinians, for instance,
placed themselves at the
disposal of the Pope, offering
preaching and confession to
the people and setting up
many foreign missions. In the 16th century St John of
the Cross and St Teresa of Avila set up a reformed
order of Carmelites – called the 'Discalced' (barefoot).
They intended to follow a stricter regime than the
original Order.

B   The number of men and women entering religious Orders has declined considerably during this century. What contribution do you think that such Orders can make to today's Catholic Church?

ANSWER IN YOUR BOOK ...

1   What is the difference between a hermit and a
    monk?

2   What is the 'Rule of St Benedict' and why do you
    think that it played such an important role in the
    monastic movement?

3   Outline some of the differences between the various
    monastic Orders.

FIND OUT AND NOTE ...

In this unit we mention the Franciscans, the
Dominicans, the Carmelites and the Augustinians. Can
you find out enough about one of these monastic
Orders to write between 500 and 600 words on them,
their beliefs and their practices?

WHAT DO YOU THINK?

a) Why do you think that men and women in the 3rd
    century began to make their way into the desert to
    dedicate themselves to God? Why do you think they
    chose the desert in particular?

b) Why do you think that each requirement of the 'Rule
    of St Benedict' was considered necessary for those
    living in a community?

c) Why do you think that some later features of the
    Catholic Church, such as the veneration of the Virgin
    Mary and penance, sprang out of the monastic
    movement?

d) Why do you think that so many Christians have
    found the monastic movement inspirational over the
    centuries?

IN THE GLOSSARY ...

Hermit; Monk; Benedictines; Nun; Abbot; Monastery;
Chastity; Franciscans; St Francis of Assissi; Disciple;
Catholic Church; Pope.

3.11 CHURCH COUNCILS

A Church Council is any official Church assembly and there have been many of them in the history of the Catholic Church. Such Councils are part of the revelatory process by which God makes his will known to his Church. There was a movement in the Middle Ages (called Conciliarism) which believed that a Council of the whole Church was superior in authority to the Pope. However, this has not been the general view of the Church. At the same time, Church Councils have been vested with considerable authority over the centuries as they have usually gathered together under the authority and inspiration of the Pope.

Among the many Church Councils in the Church's history we could mention are the following:

a) *The Nicene Council (325)*. Emperor Constantine, the first Christian Roman Emperor, summoned the Church's bishops to Nicea. This was the first ecumenical (universal) Church Council and it was called to deal with the teaching of a heretic, Arius, who was troubling the Church at the time.

b) *The Council of Ephesus (431)*. There was a fierce debate in the Church over the nature of Christ. What was most important – his divinity or humanity? The Council stressed the divinity of Jesus but undervalued his importance as a human being as a result.

c) *The Council of Chalcedon (451)*. The debate about the two natures of Christ continued. In 'The Tome of Leo' Pope Leo the Great said that the humanity and divinity were perfectly united in Christ and a new definition of orthodox belief was drawn up (called the Chalcedonian Definition).

d) *The Council of Trent (1545-63)*. The most important Church Council formed up to that time, Trent defined Catholic attitudes towards faith, marriage, the priesthood and salvation for centuries to come.

e) *The First Vatican Council (1869-70)*. This was called by Pope Pius IX to interpret and lay down the doctrine of 'Papal Infallibility' and to define the exact extent of the Pope's authority. It stressed that when the Pope is making an infallible statement, this must be fully in agreement with the teaching of the Church (the magisterium) on the subject. The Council also decided that the Church could not veto the teaching of the Pope. You will discover more about the First Vatican Council in Unit 3.12.

A *Why do you think the Catholic Church has placed such emphasis upon the meetings of Church Councils?*

f) *The Second Vatican Council (1962-65)*. This Council was summoned by Pope John XXIII with a mandate to 'open the windows of the Church and let in some fresh air'. It did just that by renewing the Church's life, liturgy and structures. It did not, however, touch any of the Catholic Church's central beliefs. Instead, it made important steps forward in defining the Catholic Church's future relationships with other Christian Churches, other religious faiths and people without faith. The Council insisted that faith is a free gift from God and all people must be free to respond to that gift in their own way. In a world where there are many religious opinions, the Church must learn to respect the consciences of those who do not, or cannot, accept the Christian faith. You will find out more about this very important Church Council in Unit 3.13.

B Although Pope John XXIII was very old when elected, he had a considerable effect on the Roman Catholic Church. Find out all that you can about him.

FIND OUT AND NOTE ...

Many people feel that the Second Vatican Council was the most important Church Council in the Catholic Church's history. Find out as much as you can about it. In particular, try to discover the following:

a) What was unusual about Pope John XXIII?

b) What did the Council say about the Church's worship?

c) What did the Council teach about Mary?

d) What did the Council encourage about the relationship between the clergy and the laity?

e) What did the Council say about salvation outside the Church?

f) To what extent have the recommendations of the Second Vatican Council been put into operation?

Keep an account of the information you have collected. This will prove useful when you cover Unit 3.13.

WHAT DO YOU THINK?

a) Why do you think that Church Councils have played such an important part in the history of the Catholic Church?

b) Why do you think that every effort has been made over the centuries to make Church Councils representative of the Church as a whole?

c) What was 'conciliarism' and how has the Church resolved the relationship between the power of the Pope and that of Church Councils? What was the contribution of the First Vatican Council to this particular debate?

ANSWER IN YOUR BOOK ...

1 What is a Church Council?

2 Why were Councils called at Nicea, Ephesus and Chalcedon?

3 Why was the Council of Trent and the First Vatican Council important?

IN THE GLOSSARY ...

Pope; Papal Infallibility; Liturgy; Bishop; Heretic; Church Council; Catholic Church; First Vatican Council; Second Vatican Council; Magisterium; Pope John XXIII.

By the middle of the 19th century there were two distinct groups which had emerged in the Catholic Church:

1 *The Conservatives*. Members of this group believed that new ideas presented the greatest challenge to the Catholic Church. New scientific ideas, such as the theory of evolution, and new approaches to the Bible had to be resisted at all costs. This group maintained that the best way to look after the Church, and keep it safe, was to strengthen the power of the Pope.

2 *The Liberals*. This group did not welcome new ideas by any means but argued that individual Catholics should have the freedom to make up their own minds.

The two groups came to the fore during the long pontificate of Pope Pius IX (1846-78). He was very much on the side of the conservatives, wanting to bring the teaching matter of all Catholic scholars under the control of the Church. As far as he was concerned the liberals were a challenge to his authority and in his famous 'Syllabus of Errors', which appeared in 1864, he summed up all the 'errors' which had occurred in recent years. Among these errors, which the Church had already condemned, were freedom of religion, progress and liberalism together with systems of government like socialism and capitalism. Any way of thinking which denied the existence of God was also condemned.

Many Catholics failed to see how the Church could set itself so firmly against a way of life which had been fought for so dearly in countries like Britain, North and South America and France. Some even left the Church as a result. At the same time the Pope proclaimed that the Virgin Mary had been 'immaculately conceived' and so had been born without sin. This was the beginning of a devotion to the Virgin Mary which remains a strong feature of the Church today.

A *What do you think the phrase 'freedom of religion' means? Why do you think that the 'Syllabus of Errors' condemned such freedom in 1864?*

These measures had been designed to strengthen the power of the Pope. This was the issue at stake when Pope Pius IX called the first Church Council to have met since the Council of Trent 300 years earlier. It was held between 1869 and 1870.

The First Vatican Council

With the 'Syllabus of Errors' still fresh in their minds the dignitaries of the Church set about strengthening the Church in the face of many challenges from outside. They did the following:

a) Rejected any ideas or systems of government, such as rationalism and naturalism, which denied that God existed.

b) Insisted on the unique and supernatural nature of the Christian revelation found in the Church's teaching and traditions. This included a denial that God spoke through any other religions or ways of thinking.

c) Settled the old quarrel as to whether Church Councils or the Pope had the final say in deciding on Church doctrine. The Council insisted that the Pope could speak

PIVS · IX · P · M ·

'infallibly' (without error) although certain conditions had to be met before any claim for this could be upheld. In particular, it was insisted that the Pope was most likely to be speaking infallibly when he was laying down the beliefs (doctrines) of the Church.

At the same time as the Council was meeting, the city of Rome passed from French to Piedmont hands. Although the Pope saw himself as a prisoner within the Vatican, Rome became the capital of the new Italian State. The Pope felt that the loss of territory was a violation of the Church but he was guaranteed recognition as the head of the Catholic Church. The Vatican was also guaranteed its own postal, telegraphic and diplomatic services. The State would not interfere with any directives from the Pope. That was the position in 1870 and it remains the position today.

B *Pope Pius IX called the First Vatican Council. What were the main recommendations of the Council and why were they considered to be necessary?*

ANSWER IN YOUR BOOK ...

1 Into which two groups did the Church become divided in the 19th century?

2 What was the 'Syllabus of Errors'?

3 What was the central concern of the First Vatican Council?

FIND OUT AND NOTE ...

a) Can you find out what socialism and capitalism are? Why do you think the Catholic Church condemned them in the middle of the 19th century?

b) Can you find out a little more about the doctrine of the Catholic Church that the Pope can, on occasions, speak of infallibly. What do you think that those who argued strongly for this at the First Vatican Council were hoping to achieve?

WHAT DO YOU THINK?

a) Why do you think that, for much of the Church's history, there has been a conflict between those who want to introduce change and those who believe that things should stay as they are?

b) Why do you think the conservatives believed that if the power of the Pope over the Church was strengthened, the Church would be protected from new ideas? Why should the Catholic Church be frightened of new ideas anyway?

IN THE GLOSSARY ...

Pope; Virgin Mary; Council of Trent.

3.13 THE SECOND VATICAN COUNCIL

Pope John XXIII was surprisingly elected Pope in 1958 at the age of seventy-seven. Most of those who elected him expected a 'caretaker' Pope who would simply look after the Catholic Church for a year or two at the most. Instead, during the five years of his reign, Pope John XXIII introduced many changes. He embraced the modern world and its technology; he became the first Pope for almost a century to travel by train; he was the first Pope in 200 years to visit the theatre and he visited hospitals and prisons.

Most important of all, Pope John XXIII called for an ecumenical Council to promote the unity of all Christian people. He declared that he wanted the Council to bring the Church into the 20th century. The Council certainly did that.

The Second Vatican Council

The Second Vatican Church Council was the 21st in the Church's history and was attended by over 3000 delegates from all parts of the world. Whereas previous Councils had been dominated by bishops from Europe, this Council drew more delegates from North and South America, Central America and Oceania – many of them being native clergy from mission churches. Representatives also attended from almost every other Christian Church although they played no part in the deliberations of the Council – at least officially.

People were dismayed when Pope John XXIII died in 1963 during the Council. His successor, Pope Paul VI, however, pledged that the Council would continue and it went through to 1965. At its conclusion, 16 documents were approved and almost all of them had an impact on the way that the Church behaved and worshipped.

The recommendations of the Second Vatican Council included the following:

a) The liturgy (services) of the Church should no longer be conducted in Latin but in the language of the people in the congregation. The participation of the people (called the laity) alongside the clergy in all parts of the liturgy was also encouraged.

b) The structure of the Church was to change. The laity and the clergy alike were seen as the 'pilgrim people of God' who were travelling along the Christian path together. Instead of an isolated Pope, the new Church would be based on the principle of 'collegiality' – the full participation of the cardinals and bishops as well as the Pope in running the Church.

c) The relationship of the Catholic Church with non-Catholic Christians was re-assessed – as were the relationships between the Catholic Church and non-Christian religions. This goal was set to bring about the eventual unity of all Christian Churches. Meanwhile, opportunities should be taken for Catholics and Protestants to work and worship together.

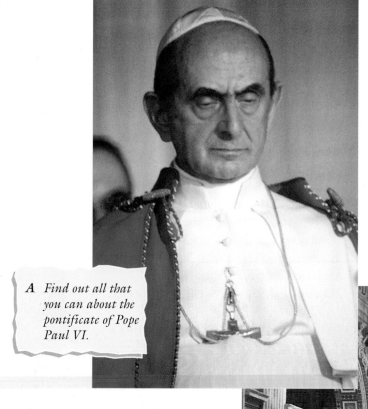

A *Find out all that you can about the pontificate of Pope Paul VI.*

72

d) Anti-semitism in any shape or form was condemned.

e) The possession of nuclear weapons and the Arms Race were condemned. So too was any move to devalue the sanctity of human life represented, for example, by abortion and euthanasia.

Pope Paul VI not only made sure that these recommendations were accepted by the Council but also took steps to ensure that they were implemented in the Church. He also welcomed opportunities to meet other Church leaders. In 1967, he met with the Orthodox Patriarch Athenagoras – the first meeting between the heads of the Roman and Eastern Churches since 1439. Talks between Anglicans and Catholics began in 1966. Talks also started up between the Catholic and Lutheran Churches.

B Why did the Second Vatican Council mark such a great step forward in the relationships between the Catholic Church and other Churches?

4.1 THE SACRAMENTS

The Catechism of 1971 links together prayer and the sacraments as the main means by which believers receive God's Grace. Prayer is the human activity by which the heart and mind are lifted up to God in adoration and praise. The sacraments, on the other hand, are given by God and are divinely ordained channels by which his blessing can reach humanity. The contribution of prayer and the sacraments to Catholic worship can be summed up in this way:

a) Prayer is humanity's contribution to its own salvation.
b) The sacraments are God's contribution to humanity's salvation.

As a consequence, the sacraments are much more important to that salvation than prayer.

What is a sacrament?

Throughout the history of the Church a sacrament has been understood as an outward and visible sign of a spiritual activity of God taking place in the soul. The Catholic Church teaches that each of the seven sacraments were ordained by Jesus Christ since he alone is able to make a physical substance the channel of God's grace.

By emphasising this truth the Church is teaching two things:

1 *Human nature is made up of two parts – the body and the soul (or spirit).*
Sometimes it is necessary to reach the soul through the body. The sacraments do this since each of them makes use of physical elements – such as bread, wine, oil and water. Each of these elements affect our senses in some way or other whether through sight, taste, touch or smell. Due to our 'humanness', God often communicates with us through our bodies.

2 *The 'Incarnation' of Jesus is the birth of God in human form.* The use of human elements in bringing us into a relationship with God is, therefore, totally appropriate. All sacraments use material elements to achieve a Divine purpose. God works through them to give a spiritual blessing which otherwise would be beyond human reach. To enjoy God's grace is to share in the life of God through which human beings can know and love him, calling him their Father.

A *While most of the sacraments make obvious use of material elements, this is slightly more obscure in the sacrament of confession. Which human element is being used here?*

How many sacraments are there?

Christians do not agree on exactly how many sacraments there are. The Salvation Army and Quakers do not celebrate any sacraments while the Anglicans recognise just two, baptism and the Eucharist. The Orthodox Church recognises seven sacraments although it prefers to call them 'mysteries'. The same seven are also acknowledged by the Catholic Church. They are as follows:

a) Baptism
b) Confirmation
c) Holy Communion
d) Penance
e) Anointing the sick
f) Ordination to the priesthood
g) Matrimony

B Can you find out which material elements are used during the sacrament of ordination to the priesthood?

What makes these sacraments so special? Just as the power of God was apparent in the life and ministry of Jesus, so it is now present in the sacraments. The sacraments are life-giving. In fact, it is the sacraments which create the Church. They reveal to mankind the mystery of that communion which is the Trinity.

ANSWER IN YOUR BOOK ...

1 What are the main means by which God's grace can be enjoyed?

2 How would you define a sacrament?

3 Can you find out why the Salvation Army and the Quakers do not celebrate any of the sacraments?

WHAT DO YOU THINK?

As we have seen, the Orthodox Church prefers to use the term 'mysteries' to describe the sacraments. To which aspect of the Sacraments does this word draw our attention to?

READ AND DECIDE ...

The CCC has the following to say:
"The purpose of the sacraments is to sanctify men, to build up the Body of Christ and, finally, to give worship to God. Because they are signs they also instruct. They not only pre-suppose faith but by words and objects they also nourish, strengthen and express it. That is why they are called the sacraments of faith." (1123)

a) Can you find out what the word 'sanctify' means?

b) In your own words, explain the three purposes of the sacraments

c) Apart from strengthening the faith of believers the sacraments also serve another purpose. What is that?

d) Why are the sacraments called 'sacraments of faith'?

IN THE GLOSSARY ...

Sacrament; Salvation Army; Quakers; Anglican Church; Orthodox Church; Baptism; Confirmation; Holy Communion; Penance; Anointing the Sick; Ordination; Matrimony; Roman Catholic Church; Priesthood; Trinity; Soul; Eucharist.

4.2 THE SACRAMENTS OF INITIATION

As the CCC points out, there was a long stage of preparation in the Early Church before a person could be admitted into the Christian Church. Only when a person had undergone this time of preparation were they admitted to the Church through the three sacraments of initiation:

a) Baptism
b) Confirmation
c) The Mass or the Eucharist

In the Early Church most catechumenates (those undergoing preparation) were adults who were making a full, and often dangerous, commitment to Christ. The three sacraments of baptism, confirmation and Communion were usually administered within the single service – the Easter Vigil.

By the 3rd century churches were being built which contained 'baptistries', into which the candidates for baptism were plunged naked, before emerging from the water as 'new born'. They were given a white garment to wear until Pentecost. This signified that they were now numbered among the 'twice-born'. They were anointed with 'chrism' (oil) before receiving the body and blood of Christ at their first Holy Communion.

Towards infant baptism

By the Middle Ages the Church had moved towards baptising babies rather than adults. The reason for this was that Europe had become largely Christian with a high rate of infant mortality (i.e. children dying before they reached their 1st birthday). By now the Church was teaching that baptism was necessary for anyone to enter heaven and parents wanted their children baptised as soon as possible. Baptism was no longer the sign of a person's own commitment to Christ. Instead, parents and the Church community had to make that commitment on the baby's behalf.

Baptism and confirmation

As the Orthodox Church separated from the Catholic Church at the Great Schism, a marked difference in practice between the two Churches emerged:

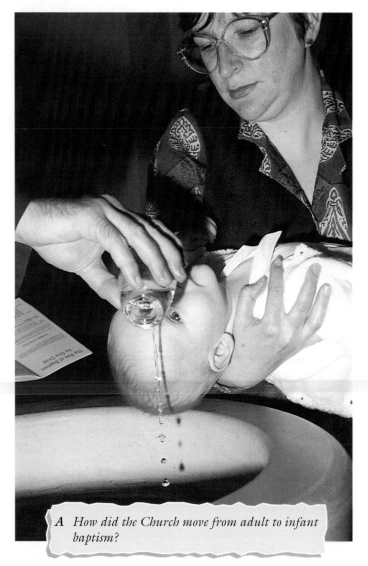

A How did the Church move from adult to infant baptism?

1   The Eastern Church, in its service of Chrismation, keeps the baptism of infants, confirmation and the first Communion together in the same service.

2   The Catholic Church, like the Anglican Church, baptises babies and then allows a lengthy time to elapse before carrying out confirmation. While infant baptism is normally carried out by a priest it can, in exceptional circumstances, be performed by a layman. Confirmation, however, is always performed by a bishop.

You will find out more about infant baptism in Unit 4.3 and Confirmation in Unit 4.4.

B *What do you think are the main arguments in favour of baptising adults rather than children?*

Adult immersion

The Second Vatican Council encouraged the Church to think more in terms of adult baptism. The Council did not question the validity of infant baptism but did underline the usefulness of adult initiation into the faith – when a person could intelligently commit themselves to Christ. It seems likely that in the future the following will happen:

a) Adult initiation, in the form of water immersion, will become more popular in the Catholic community.

b) There will be a reversion to the ancient practice of bringing the three sacraments of initiation – baptism, confirmation and communion – together into one ceremony.

ANSWER IN YOUR BOOK ...

1 What are the three sacraments of initiation in the Catholic Church?

2 Why did the Church move away from adult baptism towards the baptising of infants?

3 What do you think are the advantages of adult immersion against infant baptism?

IN YOUR OWN WORDS ...

a) What do you think is the significance of the Catholic Church having 'sacraments of initiation'? What are babies and adults being initiated into?

b) What do you think was the significance of bringing the sacraments of baptism, confirmation and communion together into one service?

c) What is the significance of the teaching of the Catholic Church that baptism is necessary before a person can enter heaven?

d) Baptism used to be seen as an expression of a person's own commitment to Jesus Christ. It has now shifted towards being a parent's profession of faith on their child's behalf? What is the significance of this?

e) Do you think the fact that a priest or a laymen can conduct a baptism, while a bishop always carries out the service of confirmation, has any significance? If so, what might it be?

IN THE GLOSSARY ...

Sacrament; Baptism; Confirmation; Mass; Eucharist; Holy Communion; Heaven; Bishop; Priest; Chrismation; Pentecost; Infant baptism; Catholic Church; Orthodox Church; Great Schism; Anglican Church; Second Vatican Council.

4.3 INFANT BAPTISM

Whether they are baptised as children or adults, baptism is the first sacrament that Catholics receive – opening the door to all the others. Infant baptism remains the norm within the Catholic Church. Like all other sacraments, this is invalid without faith. This faith is not demanded of the infant but is supplied by the parents of the child concerned and by the whole church community.

The priest presides over infant baptism in his capacity as the representative of God and the whole church family. When he greets the parents and child at the door of the church he is welcoming them into the family of faith. The service which follows usually, but not always, takes the form of a Mass.

There are several distinct stages in the service of infant baptism and each one of them is important:

a) The priest begins by asking the parents for the child's name. To call a child by its name underlines his or her uniqueness in the sight of God, who knows all of us by our own names. The tradition is that one of the child's names should be that of a saint, to underline the Catholic belief that the child is joining the 'communion of saints', which embraces all believers – alive and dead.

b) The parents and godparents are asked questions to determine whether they are taking the service of baptism seriously. They are reminded that in bringing their child to be baptised they are indicating their own willingness to bring him or her up in the Catholic faith. The priest then welcomes the child into the church family:

> "N, the Christian community welcomes you with great joy. In its name I claim you for Christ our Saviour by the sign of his cross. I now trace the cross on your forehead and invite your parents and godparents to do the same."

c) The Liturgy of the Word (the reading of the Holy Scriptures) then follows. If the baptism takes place on a Sunday or an important feast day the readings are taken from the Lectionary. They are likely to include passages from the Old Testament and the Epistles as well as the Gospels. These are followed by a homily (talk) and the 'Prayers of the Faithful' (Bidding prayers). The Liturgy ends with the 'Litany of the Saints'.

d) The part of the service in which Satan is exorcised follows. This takes place before the baby is anointed

A *What do you think are the responsibilities of Catholic parents towards their children?*

with oil (the Oil of Catechumens). This oil is used in many acts of Catholic worship, symbolising the healing and strength of God. The priest reinforces this by 'laying his hands' on the child, calling upon the blessing of God.

e) After the water has been blessed and the parents and godparents make their final confession of faith, the priest baptises the baby 'in the name of the Father, and of the Son and of the Holy Spirit.' In baptism it is recognised that:

"God is our Father (Abba),
Jesus is our brother,
The Holy Spirit lives within us."

Finally, the baby is anointed with 'chrism' (consecrated oil); the parents are presented with a candle which is lit from the Paschal Candle; a white

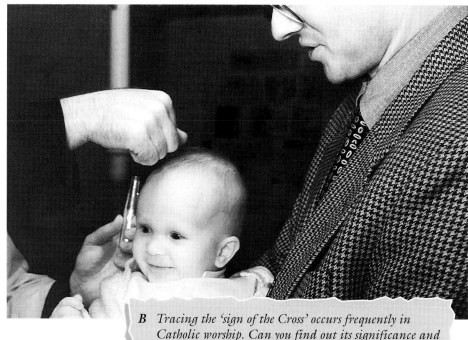

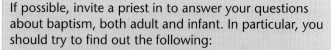

B Tracing the 'sign of the Cross' occurs frequently in Catholic worship. Can you find out its significance and some of the other occasions on which it occurs.

shawl (to represent the child's garment of new life) is placed around the baby and the family is blessed by the priest.

ANSWER IN YOUR BOOK ...

1 What is the 'Liturgy of the Word'?

2 Why is the baby anointed with oil in baptism?

3 How does the priest indicate that the baby is special both in the sight of God and in the eyes of the Church?

DISCUSS AMONG YOURSELVES ...

Here are three issues connected with infant baptism for you to think about:

a) On a few occasions a priest might refuse to baptise a baby. What do you think these occasions might be and is the priest right to withold his consent?

b) Can you find out about, and then discuss together, the qualities and responsibilities of being a godparent?

c) In many parishes children are now brought forward to baptism during the Mass. Can you think of two reasons why this is happening? Do you think it is a practice that should be encouraged?

FIND OUT AND NOTE ...

If possible, invite a priest in to answer your questions about baptism, both adult and infant. In particular, you should try to find out the following:

a) Why did the Church turn to infant baptism after originally practising adult baptism? Why is it now trying to return, in part, to adult immersion?

b) What does the Church actually believe happens when a baby is baptised? Does any 'change' take place within the child or is it all symbolic? If it is symbolic, what does the actual symbolism represent?

c) How does the Church believe that other people, in this case parents and godparents, can exercise faith on behalf of young babies?

IN THE GLOSSARY ...

Infant Baptism; Sacrament; Mass; Priest; Saint; Communion of Saints; Sign of the Cross; Liturgy; Holy Scriptures; Holy Spirit; Laying on of hands.

4.4 CONFIRMATION

In the Acts of the Apostles we learn of Christians in Samaria who had been baptised but were yet to receive the Holy Spirit. As Luke tells us:

> "...as yet he (the Holy Spirit) had not come down on any of them: they had only been baptised in the name of the Lord Jesus. Then they laid hands on them and they received the Holy Spirit."
> (Acts 8.16, 17)

This suggests that, from the very beginning, the gift of the Holy Spirit was given in addition to baptism. This the Church calls 'Confirmation'.

As we saw in Unit 4.2, baptism and confirmation are both 'sacraments of initiation' which belong to the beginning of a person's Christian pilgrimage. Even if they are separated by a lengthy period of time, as they are in the Catholic Church, they should be seen as part of the one sacrament.

Confirmation in the Catholic Church

In the Catholic Church, as in the Anglican Church, the two sacraments have been separate for centuries.

Catholics believe that the Holy Spirit is given to a baby when he or she is baptised. The Christian life, though, is one of growth and the vows which others took on the baby's behalf when it was baptised now have to be renewed. The difference is that confirmation only takes place when a person can renew those vows, and their Christian commitment, for themselves. In practice, this is likely to mean that a person is confirmed sometime between their 12th and 14th birthdays. If someone is converted to Catholicism later, however, they can be confirmed at any age. Whatever their age, confirmation is always preceded by a long period of instruction by the parish priest.

The sacrament of confirmation is usually carried out by the area bishop and this underlines the importance which the Church attaches to it. It takes place within the central service of the Mass and follows the Liturgy of the Word. As the Mass is a celebration of our unity with God and with each other, so it is the right place for people to come into a full relationship with God and his family.

A The 'laying on of hands' is a traditional Church practice and an important part of the Confirmation service. Can you find out anything about it? In which other services is it used?

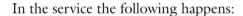

B Why does the Catholic Church ask these children to wait until they are teenagers before they are confirmed?

In the service the following happens:

a) Those being confirmed are asked to renew their baptismal promises. They affirm their own faith by repeating the words of the Apostles Creed.

b) The bishop, and any priests involved in the service, place their hands gently on the heads of each confirmation candidate.

c) The bishop administers the Sacrament of Confirmation when he traces the 'sign of the cross' on each forehead with oil (chrism). As he does so he says:

"N, be sealed with the Gift of the Holy Spirit."

The person responds with 'Amen' to show that he or she has accepted the sacrament from the bishop's hands.

d) Following the Peace, the Prayers of the Faithful and the Lord's Prayer, the person confirmed takes Holy Communion. The Eucharist celebrates our union both with God and with each other so Catholics receive the elements of bread and wine every time they go to Mass. It is especially important, however, to receive them after they have been confirmed as this brings together the sacraments of initiation (baptism, confirmation and communion).

The initiation of the person into the Church fellowship is now complete and they are committed to serve God in the world. This is why the final blessing of the bishop contains the words:

'May he bless you and give you courage in professing the true faith.'

READ AND DECIDE ...

After he has laid his hands on the confirmation candidates the bishop prays:
"All-powerful God, Father of our Lord Jesus Christ,
by water and the Holy Spirit,
you freed your sons and daughters from sin,
and gave them new life.
Send your Holy Spirit upon them
to be their helper and guide.
Give them the spirit of wisdom and understanding,
the spirit of right judgement and courage,
the spirit of knowledge and reverence.
Fill them with the spirit of wonder and awe in your presence,
We ask this through Christ our Lord. Amen."

This is such an important prayer that it is worth learning. After you have done this, try to answer the following:

a) Through which means has God freed his sons and daughters from sin?

b) In your own words, describe the gifts that the Holy Spirit brings.

c) What do you understand by the words 'Fill them with the spirit of wonder and awe in your presence.'?

ANSWER IN YOUR BOOK ...

1 What is the link between baptism and confirmation?
2 What lies at the heart of the service of confirmation?
3 Can you explain why it is important for a person to take Holy Communion after they have been confirmed?

IN THE GLOSSARY ...

Sacrament; Baptism; Confirmation; Orthodox Church; New Testament; Chrismation; Catholic Church; Anglican Church; Holy Spirit; Mass; Apostles Creed; Peace; Lord's Prayer; Priest; Eucharist; Bishop; Sign of the Cross; Acts of the Apostles; Liturgy.

4.5 THE EUCHARIST

Like baptism, the Eucharist, or the Lord's Supper (the term used in the oldest account of the sacrament recorded in 1.Corinthians 11.20) is rooted firmly in the very beginnings of the Church. The tradition of the Last Supper is found in four different places in the New Testament:

❖ 1.Corinthians 11.23-25
❖ Mark 14.22-25
❖ Matthew 26.26-29
❖ Luke 22.15-20

Read each of these accounts through carefully.

The Last Supper

In the time of Jesus, shared meals were more than a simple device for eating. They symbolically demonstrated peace, trust and a sense of community. In fact, they took on an almost holy or sacred meaning. They were a time for sharing God's goodness with friends. To be invited to share a meal with someone was a sign of a deep friendship. Jesus, though, broke this convention by sharing many meals with the outcasts of his day (tax-collectors and prostitutes among them). This was a sign that the Kingdom of God had begun. The people were looking forward to this time but some, particularly the religious leaders, could not come to terms with the fact that it was more likely to be welcomed by those who were rejected by society.

Jesus shared the Last Supper with his disciples. It was either the meal eaten at the start of the Jewish feast of Passover or the meal that was traditionally eaten on the evening before the festival began. Whichever one of these it was, the meal was eaten in the knowledge that God's Kingdom was still to come in its entirety.

The structure of the Last Supper was taken from the Jewish Passover meal – the words said over the bread, the breaking and sharing of the bread and the blessing over the wine. Jesus, though, introduced a new and very distinctive element. It was to be his body which was to be broken and his blood which was to be poured out to pay for the sins of the world and to establish a new covenant between God and the people.

By sharing his body and blood with his disciples, Jesus revealed to them that sacrifice which shortly was going to take place at Calvary. The idea of communicating divine gifts through the simple necessities of eating and drinking was familiar to all of them.

After Jesus rose from the dead his disciples often met again for these communal meals. Now, though, there was another factor. They were convinced that the risen Christ, through the Holy Spirit, was present with them (Matthew 18.20). By meeting together they were carrying out the wishes of the Lord. The meal that they shared together became the re-enactment of the last meal they shared with Jesus. Every time the Church celebrates the Mass, this re-enactment is continued.

A What do you think a family might gain from regularly eating together? Why do you think that such meals were particularly important in the time of Jesus?

82

B How does the Mass reflect the last meal that Jesus shared with his disciples?

ANSWER IN YOUR BOOK ...

1 What can be learned from the New Testament about the institution of the Eucharist?

2 What did the last meal shared by Jesus with his disciples owe to the Jewish faith?

3 Can you explain the link between the Church's celebration of the Mass and the Last Supper?

READ AND DECIDE ...

a) In John's Gospel two extended passages have a close link with the Last Supper. They are:
   ❖ 6.1-15
   ❖ 6.22-5

   Read them through carefully and note down any phrases or elements which remind you of the Last Supper. Is there anything in these passages which might throw some light on the last meal which Jesus ate with his disciples or the subsequent feast of the Eucharist?

b) The story of the Last Supper includes the treachery of Judas Iscariot (Luke 22.21-23). Why do you think Judas chose this occasion to set his treachery into motion? How do you think the other disciples, and later the early Christians, would have reacted to the story of Judas leaving the meal to betray Christ? Is there anything in the story which might help people today to understand the Eucharist better?

CAN YOU EXPLAIN?

a) Can you explain the link between the Last Supper which Jesus enjoyed with his disciples and the celebration of the Mass within the Church today?

b) Can you explain, in around 500 words, the way in which Jesus used a meal and the common elements of bread and wine to set up a celebration of his forthcoming death?

IN THE GLOSSARY ...

Baptism; Eucharist; Lord's Supper; Church; Last Supper; New Testament; Holy Spirit; Kingdom of God; Passover; Mass; Sacrament; Disciple.

4.6 CELEBRATING THE MASS

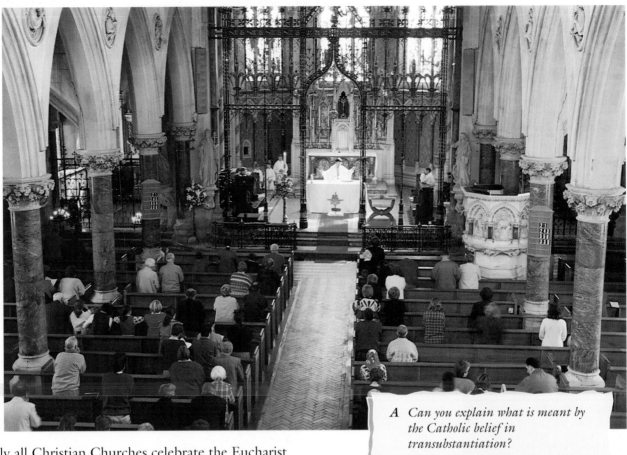

A *Can you explain what is meant by the Catholic belief in transubstantiation?*

Nearly all Christian Churches celebrate the Eucharist although the emphasis and meaning that they attach to this celebration varies considerably. The Eucharist is the most important sacrament because Christ is present in it even before it is shared. It is the summit to which the Christian life aspires and the source of the most important Christian blessings.

Terms and Meanings

The 'Eucharist' is a term which Roman Catholics share with Anglicans. This comes from a Greek word meaning 'thanksgiving' and draws attention to the fact that believers receive spiritual benefits in this meal from God, for which they give their praise. In the Roman Catholic Church, however, the term 'Mass' is more likely to be used. The actual origin of this word is somewhat obscure but probably comes from the very last words of the old Latin Mass – 'Ite Missa est' ('Go, it is ended').

There are two beliefs underlying the Mass which distinguish Roman Catholics from most Protestants. They are:

1 That the Mass is in some way a sacrifice. In it Christ renews the original, voluntary sacrifice of his life to God for the sins of the world. Through the Mass he makes that sacrifice present for all worshippers;

2 That the bread and wine change, when they are consecrated in the Mass, into the body and blood of Christ.

This belief, one of the real distinguishing marks between Roman Catholics and Protestants, is called 'transubstantiation'. The Eucharist is different to all other sacraments in one way. During the sacrament the 'Real Presence' of Christ is present in the bread and wine.

The Mass itself

The priest begins Mass by making the sign of the cross and leading the people in their repentance before God. On every Sunday, apart from those in Advent and Lent, the Gloria ("Glory to God in the highest and peace to his people on earth") is either said or sung. The following then happens:

a) The Liturgy of the Word takes place. This includes readings from the Old Testament, Epistles and Gospels as well as a homily from the priest.

b) The gifts of bread and wine are then brought to the altar by representatives of the congregation. Having offered two 'blessing' prayers the priest washes his hands to symbolise his cleansing before he offers the sacrifice of the Mass.

c) The 'Eucharistic Prayer' is the centre of the celebration. Although several different prayers can be used their essence is the same: Jesus took bread, gave thanks, blessed it, broke it and gave it to his friends. Through the Holy Spirit the priest asks that the bread and wine might become the body and blood of Jesus.

d) The Peace is then followed by the breaking and sharing of bread. As the priest holds up the host he invites the people to receive the gift which God has given with the words:

"This is the Lamb of God
who takes away the sins of the world.
Happy are those who are called to his supper."

B *What is meant by the 'Real Presence'?*

To this, the people reply:

"Lord, I am not worthy to receive you,
but only say the word and I shall be healed."

Before the Eucharist finishes one final act remains. The priest asks God that the Eucharist may change the lives of the people. He then dismisses them with the words:

"Go in peace to love and serve the Lord."

READ AND DECIDE ...

St Paul wrote:
"The fact that there is only one loaf means that, though there are many of us, we form a single body because we all have a share in this single loaf." (1.Corinthians. 10.17)

a) What point do you think Paul is making about the symbolic importance of the Eucharist?

b) How does the Peace in the Eucharist underline the belief that all are one in this sacrament?

c) How does the Eucharist underline the belief that all Christians should work together for peace and justice in the world?

ANSWER IN YOUR BOOK ...

1 Can you explain the meaning of the words 'Eucharist' and 'Mass'?

2 What is the 'Liturgy of the Word'?

3 What happens during the 'Prayer of Consecration'?

WHAT DO YOU THINK?

The homily given during the Mass is described as the 'breaking of the bread of the Word'. Try to explain what you think this phrase might mean.

IN THE GLOSSARY ...

Priest; Sign of the Cross; Old Testament; Gospel; Epistles; Altar; Eucharist; Sacrament; Liturgy; Priest; Mass; Protestant; Transubstantiation; Sunday; Advent; Lent; Holy Spirit; Peace.

4.7 PENANCE AND RECONCILIATION

A person becomes a member of the Catholic community through baptism and confirmation. This, however, is only the beginning of a long process. Human beings are prone to sin and such sin is:

> "…an offence against God, a rupture of communion with him. At the same time it damages communion with the Church." (CCC 1440)

As a result, human beings are faced with a paradox. They are called to be 'perfect' and yet become increasingly aware of their imperfections or sins. For this reason, the Church offers the sacrament of penance and reconciliation (confession).

The new rite of penance

Although this sacrament has been practised by the Church for centuries it was given a new focus by the Second Vatican Council. This Council declared that its purpose was to obtain "pardon from the mercy of God" and to be:

> "reconciled with the Church whom (sinners) have wounded by their sin, and who, by its charity, its example and prayer, collaborates in their conversion." (Dogmatic Constitution on the Church. n.11)

In the 17th century the 'confessional box' was introduced to ensure the privacy of penitents. Confession became concerned with confessing sin and receiving absolution from the priest. There was little emphasis upon developing a relationship with the priest and, through him, forging a closer relationship with God. The Second Vatican Council, however, opened the way for face-to-face conversations with a priest, allowing the person to receive more direct help and counselling. Although the priest now knows the identity of the penitent he is still bound by the 'seal of confession', which means that he cannot reveal to anyone what has been said during the course of a confession.

In the act of making a confession the following happens:

a) The penitent is reminded by the priest that God will always forgive the person who is genuinely sorry for their sins. The priest will probably read a passage from the Bible to underline this.

b) When the penitent has confessed their sin(s) the priest offers them a few words of advice and encouragement. He then suggests a penance, such as the saying of a few simple prayers, so that the person can show God that they are genuinely sorry for their actions.

c) Once confession has been made and the penance accepted the 'act of sorrow' takes place. Forgiveness is only available to those people who:

A This person is receiving absolution but what does that mean?

❖ show that they are are genuinely sorry for their past actions (contrition);

❖ show that they are determined to change their lives in the future (a firm purpose of amendment).

d) The priest then uses the ministry of forgiveness, a ministry which Jesus gave to his Church. It is not the priest who forgives the penitent but God. The priest merely offers a visible symbol that such forgiveness is given. This he does either by placing his hands on the penitent or by raising his right hand as he pronounces the Absolution. The person replies 'Amen' and the sacrament of penance is given. The sign of the cross is made over the person as the priest says:

"I absolve you from your sins in the name of the Father, and of the Son and of the Holy Spirit."

This reminds the penitent that it is through the sacrifice of Jesus on the cross that he or she has been released from the guilt and punishment of their sins. Through the Sacrament of Reconciliation the baptismal relationship between God and the person has been restored.

ANSWER IN YOUR BOOK ...

1 What part does the Sacrament of Reconciliation play in the life of the Christian?

2 What change in the sacrament was brought about by the Second Vatican Council.

3 What events lead up to the pronouncement of absolution by the priest?

READ AND DECIDE ...

This is the prayer of absolution:

"God, the Father of mercies, through the death and resurrection of his Son had reconciled the world to himself and sent the Holy Spirit among us for the forgiveness of sins; through the ministry of the Church may God give you pardon and peace, and I absolve you from your sins in the name of the Father, and of the Son and of the Holy Spirit."

a) When the priest calls God 'the Father of mercies' what do you think he means?

b) How has God shown that he is willing to forgive the sins of those who confess?

c) What part does the Church play in the process of forgiveness?

WHAT DO YOU THINK?

In the time of Jesus the disease of leprosy was always used as a symbol for sin. With this in mind, read Mark 1.40-45. What do you think this particular episode in the life of Jesus might teach us about sin and forgiveness?

IN THE GLOSSARY ...

Penance; Confession; Second Vatican Council; Priest; Bible; Baptism; Confirmation; Sacrament; Confessional box; Absolution; Sign of the Cross.

4.8 ANOINTING THE SICK

Until Pope Paul VI publicly announced the new rite of anointing the sick in 1972, the Church had been unsure about the practice. He introduced a sacrament which involves far more than just praying for the recovery of someone who is ill. It also comprises of the following:

1 An assurance to the sick person that they are not alone in their suffering. This assurance comes from two directions:
   ❖ they are supported by God's love;
   ❖ they are encouraged by the activity of the praying Christian community.

A Why is the Pope laying his hands on this sick person?

2 A reassurance that God has not forgotten or abandoned them. There are times when a person who is seriously ill will, almost inevitably, be tempted to doubt that God is with them. The sacrament of anointing assures them that He is.

3 A celebration of the fact that through suffering, the person is sharing in the sufferings of Christ and playing a part in the redemption of the world.

The Sacrament of anointing

There are three main parts to the sacrament:

a) Before turning to the Bible the priest often sprinkles the sick person, and anyone else present, with holy water. The water is a reminder that the person first started to follow Jesus through baptism, shared in his redemption through the Eucharist and is now sharing in his suffering. Bible readings are followed by prayers in which God is asked to forgive and heal the sick person. In silence the priest lays his hands on the sick person, reminding him or her that Jesus often laid his hands on those who were sick prior to healing them.

b) The priest brings with him some olive oil which has been blessed by the bishop at the Chrism Mass, held in the Cathedral Church of every diocese on Maundy Thursday. At this ceremony three kinds of oil are blessed:`
   ❖ the oil of catechumens – used at baptism;
   ❖ the oil of chrism – used in baptism and confirmation;
   ❖ the oil of the sick.

Using the oil, the priest anoints the forehead and hands of the sick person. The oil symbolises healing and strength. The priest says a prayer which speaks of the person's condition – whether they are seriously ill, dying etc. The 'Our Father' is recited since this prayer addresses all needs and conditions. In particular, it reminds the sick person that God is their Father in heaven who loves and cares for them.

c) Wherever possible, the sacrament of anointing the sick is combined with the taking of Holy Communion. Whenever this sacrament is celebrated, the believer is united with God in a special way. Suffering draws the believer even closer to God. As the host is held up by the priest those present are invited to trust in God's love. If the person receiving communion is dying and this may be the last communion they take, the communion itself is called 'viaticum'. While the service is similar to that of anointing the sick, the person is reminded of their baptismal promises and assured that they are travelling to their Father in heaven.

B *What is the significance of the priest anointing the sick person?*

ANSWER IN YOUR BOOK ...

1 What lies behind the sacrament of anointing the sick?

2 What are the three main parts to the sacrament of anointing the sick?

3 What is the Viaticum?

CAN YOU EXPLAIN?

Can you explain the symbolic importance of the following in the sacrament of anointing the sick?

a) Sprinkling the person with holy water?

b) Laying hands on the sick person?

c) Anointing the sick person with oil?

READ AND DECIDE ...

The only reference in the New Testament to the practice of anointing the sick with oil is found in James 5.15,16:

"If one of you is ill, he should send for the elders of the church, and they must anoint him with oil in the name of the Lord and pray over him. The prayer of faith will save the sick man and the Lord will raise him up again; if he has committed any sins he will be forgiven. So confess your sins to one another…"

a) Why do you think the elders of the church are entrusted with anointing the sick person?

b) Can you find out why oil was believed to have such curative properties?

c) What is it that will save the sick man?

d) What is the suggested connection between sickness and sin in this quotation?

IN THE GLOSSARY ...

Sacrament; Bible; Chrism; Viaticum; Baptism; Eucharist; Our Father; Priest; Maundy Thursday; Holy Communion; Laying on of hands; Bishop; Mass; Diocese; Confirmation.

4.9 ORDINATION

As we have seen the Second Vatican Council stressed that all believers, ordained and lay-persons, were called to be 'priests'. It does require, however, a special vocation to be called to serve God through ordination. The Catholic Church spends a long time 'testing the vocation' of those who believe that they should become priests. Within ordination there are three 'orders': bishops (episcopate); clergy (presbyterate) and deacons.

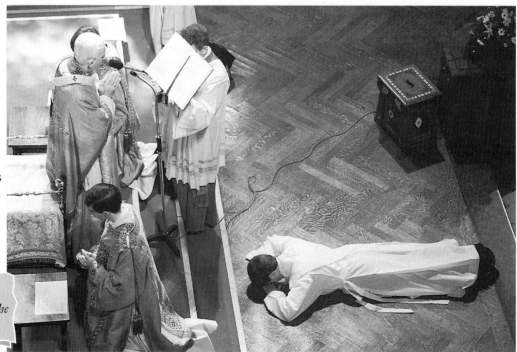

A *This bishop is being consecrated by the laying on of hands. Why is this an important part of the consecration service?*

By the end of the first century, bishops were the authority within the Christian community and they alone could celebrate the sacraments. The source of their authority came from the original Apostles through 'the laying on of hands' (apostolic succession). This was underlined by the Second Vatican Council:

"From the earliest days of the Church the first place has always been accorded to the bishops because of the life-giving contact between them and the apostles, because of the unbroken succession that links them."

Bishops

Sometime between the time of Paul and the end of the first century, bishops became an important part of the Church. While Paul, in his letter to Titus, (Refer to **READ AND DECIDE...**) talks of 'elders' as the Church leaders, by 100 CE St Ignatius writes about the control that bishops exercise over the running of the Church:

"No-one should do anything that pertains to the Church without the bishop's permission. The only proper Eucharist is one which is celebrated by the bishop or one of his representatives."

B *Why do you think a priest prostrates himself in front of the bishop during his ordination?*

As long as the Christian community remained small the bishops could retain such power in their own hands. As the Church spread, however, so the work of the 'presbyter', or priest, developed.

Consecration to the priesthood

When he is ordained as a deacon, a man takes a vow of perpetual celibacy. Twelve months later, he sits among the people that he will serve as he is ordained to the priesthood. The bishop confirms the Church's acceptance of the person's call to the ministry. As the candidate kneels he places his hands between those of the bishop as the two of them agree to work together in the service of the Church. The bishop then invites the whole congregation to pray for the priest as he prostrates himself, face downwards, on the floor.

As the moment of ordination approaches the candidate kneels before the bishop, who lays his hands on the candidate's head. The bishop is indicating that the person has received the gift of the Holy Spirit which will make them a priest. The priest is ordained by the bishop, saying the Prayer of Consecration. The new priest puts on the vestments of the priesthood – the stole and the chasuble. His hands are anointed with oil before he is presented to the people and the bishop hands him the elements of bread and wine. The most important part of his future ministry will be to preside over the Eucharist. He will also be expected to set the people a clear example by the quality of his spiritual life. He can only do this through God's strength and so his ordination ends when he offers the Peace to the bishop and other priests in the congregation.

ANSWER IN YOUR BOOK ...

1 How did the Order of Bishops develop in the Church?

2 Why do you think that the doctrine of 'Apostolic Succession' is very important to the Church?

3 What happens during the service of ordination to indicate that a call to the priesthood is very special?

READ AND DECIDE ...

In his letter to Titus Paul described the qualities that an 'elder' in the Church should have:

"...each of them must be a man of irreproachable character; he must not have been married more than once, and his children must be believers and not uncontrollable or liable to be charged with disorderly conduct...he must be irreproachable: never an arrogant or hot-tempered man, nor a heavy drinker or violent, nor out to make money but a man who is hospitable and a friend of all that is good; sensible, moral, devout and self-controlled; and he must have a firm grasp of the unchanging message of the tradition..." (Titus 1.6-9)

a) Are any of the characteristics demanded of an elder surprising?

b) Why do you think that an elder is judged not only by his own conduct but by that of his family as well?

c) The issue of the family highlights one difference between a bishop in the Catholic Church and an elder in Paul's day. How would you explain that difference?

WHAT DO YOU THINK?

St Paul was celibate – unmarried. At the time, this was seen as a special gift from God to the Church and it was not until the 12th century that it was made compulsory for all priests. Today it is questioned by many, both inside and outside the Church. What do you think are the main arguments for and against celibacy? Can you see a time when celibacy will no longer be compulsory for priests?

IN THE GLOSSARY ...

Second Vatican Council; Episcopacy; Bishop; Clergy; Ordination; Vocation; Catholic Church; St Paul; Church; Eucharist; Laying on of hands; Priesthood; Holy Spirit; Eucharist; Deacon; Sacrament; Apostle; Apostolic Succession; Priest; Celibacy; Peace.

4.10 HOLY ORDERS

Through the laying on of a bishop's hands, the sacrament of Holy Orders is conferred on a man who has responded to his vocation. Through this sacrament, three orders within the Church can be conferred – that of bishop, priest or deacon. Why, though, are they called 'Holy Orders'?

1 They are 'holy' because the vocations conferred are not just administrative tasks within the Church. Each person ordained shares in the priesthood of Jesus.
2 They are 'Orders' because, in the hierarchy of the Church, these are the three main 'callings' or 'vocations'.

There is also another important element in this sacrament. Just like the sacraments of baptism and confirmation, Holy Orders convey a kind of 'character' on the recipient. He receives power and authority from God to carry out his important work. Unlike the other two, however, this is not a blessing given to him for his own spiritual growth but one that he will be expected to impart to others for the whole of his ministry.

The authority of the priest

In Roman Catholicism the priesthood can be understood in two ways:

1 The whole Church forms a 'priestly people' with every baptised member given the task of making Christ known to the world.

2 Within the Church fellowship some people are called to that 'special priesthood' which is only enjoyed by those who have been ordained. Just as the ordained priesthood makes special demands on a person so they are given a spiritual power which is not experienced by ordinary Christians. This special power enables a priest to do the following:

   a) Preside over the changing of the bread and wine into the body and blood of Jesus during the Eucharist. This very important role can only be carried out by those who are authorised and ordained by the Church.
   b) Dispense the other sacraments. In most of these

the priest alone can officiate. There are two exceptions to this rule:

❖ in infant baptism any lay person can carry out the sacrament in an emergenecy;
❖ in matrimony the husband and wife bestow the sacrament on one another.

   c) Act as the special representative of Jesus Christ. Through ordination, Jesus Christ himself sets apart a priest for his holy work. Within the Roman Catholic tradition, therefore, the priest carries an authority which is not shared by the priests, ministers or pastors of any other Christian denomination.

A What authority does a priest have which is not given to an ordinary Catholic?

B The Anglican Church ordained its first women in the UK in 1994. Can you see a time when this will happen in the Roman Catholic Church as well?

d) Be the special mediator between God and man. This is the role of the priest when he dispenses the various sacraments. He offers sacrifice to God on behalf of the Church and bestows blessings on the Church from God through the sacraments.

Women priests

Women are not admitted to the priesthood in the Roman Catholic Church. The Congregation for the Doctrine of the Faith, reporting in 1976, declared that:

> "The Church, in fidelity to the example of the Lord, does not consider herself authorised to admit women to priestly ordination."

Jesus did not appoint any women as apostles. Paul taught that women were not permitted even to speak in church (1.Corinthians 14.33) nor to exercise any authority over a man (1.Timothy 2.12). In the centuries that followed, this rule was followed without exception. The present Pope, John Paul *II*, has announced that it will continue.

READ AND DECIDE ...

Here are three quotations about the priesthood. Read them carefully before answering the questions:

a) "Let everyone revere the deacons as Jesus Christ, the bishop as the image of the Father, and the presbyters (priests) as the senate of God and the assembly of the apostles. For without them one cannot speak of the Church."
(Ignatius, 2nd century)
❖ What do you think the word 'revere' means?

b) "Through the sacrament of Holy Orders priests share in the universal dimensions of the mission Christ entrusted to the apostles."(CCC 1565)
❖ After reading Matthew 28.19,20, can you explain what the" ...universal dimensions of the mission Christ entrusted to his apostles" are?

c) "Because it is joined with the episcopal order the office of priest shares in the authority by which Christ himself builds up and sanctifies and rules his Body." (CCC 1567)
❖ What is the 'episcopacy'? What special 'authority' does a priest have?

ANSWER IN YOUR BOOK ...

1 What are 'Holy Orders'?
2 What is the main difference between someone in Holy Orders and an ordinary Catholic?
3 What does ordination to the priesthood enable someone to do?

IN THE GLOSSARY ...

Bishop; Laying on of Hands; Priest; Deacon; Sacrament; Baptism; Confirmation; Priesthood; Eucharist; Matrimony; Minister; Catholic Church; Apostle; Vocation; Infant Baptism; Ordination; St Paul; Pope.

4.11 MATRIMONY

Every Christian Church attaches the greatest importance to marriage (matrimony). In the Roman Catholic and Orthodox Churches, however, it is a sacrament. It is seen as a sign of God's love among his people. To share in the sacrament of marriage is to participate in that part of God which is found in all human love.

The Sacrament of Marriage

There are two ways in which the marriage ceremony can be celebrated in a Catholic church:

a) The marriage can be consecrated as part of a special Mass – called a 'Nuptial Mass'. This is usually the case when two Catholics are marrying each other since, through the Mass, they offer their future lives together to God.

b) There can be a simple ceremony of marriage without a Mass.

As the service begins the bride and groom join each other in the sanctuary – a recent practice. It symbolically shows that the man and the woman are 'priests' together since they will offer the sacrament of matrimony to each other. After welcoming them the priest leads the way into the Liturgy of the Word. The couple choose the passages to be read from the Bible and, apart from the Gospel passage, which is always read by a priest or deacon, these are usually read by relatives or friends.

Three questions are directed at the couple to see whether they are prepared to commit themselves fully to each other and to God's gift of children. If they

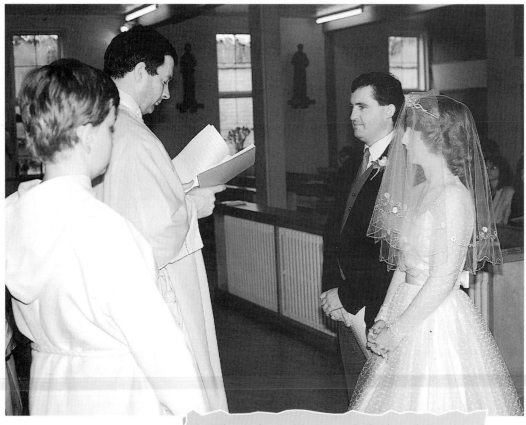

A *What is the significance of the bride and groom offering the sacrament of matrimony to each other?*

cannot answer the questions truthfully, the ensuing marriage is not valid in the eyes of God or the Church. The couple must freely assent to the marriage before they exchange their vows. These vows, or promises, are the same as couples make in many other Churches. The priest ends with the familiar words:

"What God has joined together, let no man put asunder."

The Church takes this to mean that the marriage which is now being made in the sight of God cannot be dissolved (see Unit 7.4). The permanence of the marriage is symbolised by the ring that the groom places on his bride's finger. Having been blessed by the priest this ring becomes sacred. It is a constant reminder of the love that they have for each other, a love in which God is always present.

The Bidding Prayers are then offered for the Church and the world. Obviously, these prayers focus on the couple's future together. If there is a Mass as part of the wedding celebration, this then follows. If not, a Nuptial Blessing is pronounced. This is a special prayer for those who are newly married. With the Peace the sacrament ends.

B *Many parishes now undertake a lengthy period of instruction before marriage. What help do you think the Church can give a couple looking forward to getting married?*

ANSWER IN YOUR BOOK ...

1 Why does the Catholic Church consider marriage to be a sacrament?

2 How does the sacrament of marriage stand out from other sacraments?

3 What is the spiritual significance of the ring?

READ AND DECIDE ...

In reminding the couple of the background to marriage, a priest introduces many important elements in the Christian approach to marriage:"

"N and N, you have come together in this church so that the Lord may seal and strengthen your love in the presence of the Church's minister and this community. Christ abundantly blesses this love. He has already consecrated you in baptism and now he enriches and strengthens you by a special sacrament so that you may assume the duties of marriage in mutual and lasting fidelity."

a) How is God present in the love between two people? How is this celebrated in the sacrament of marriage?

b) What does the public celebration of their love openly demonstrate?

c) What is the link between the sacraments of baptism and marriage?

WHAT DO YOU THINK?

During the service three questions are asked of the bride and groom. Think about these and their implications carefully:

a) "Are you ready freely and without reservation to give yourselves to each other in marriage?"
   ❖ What do you think lies behind this question? What are its implications?

b) "Are you ready to love and honour each other as man and wife for the rest of your life?"
   ❖ Do you think it is possible for a man and a woman to promise 'to love and honour' one another for the rest of their lives?

c) "Are you ready to accept children lovingly from God and bring them up according to the law of Christ and his Church?"
   ❖ Where do you think that having children fits into the reasons for marriage? Where does this particular question leave those couples who are unable to have children?

IN THE GLOSSARY ...

Catholic Church; Orthodox Church; Sacrament; Mass; Priest; Bible; Deacon; Liturgy; Gospels; Peace.

5.1 A CATHOLIC CHURCH

Traditionally, Roman Catholic churches were built in the shape of a cross or an oblong, but many of the newer ones are circular, to stress the equality of all the people as they worship in God's house. In such places of worship as the Cathedral of Christ the King in Liverpool and Clifton Cathedral in Bristol, the people either surround the altar or sit in a semi-circle in front of it. In both cases the intended symbolism is clear. The altar is the place where God meets with his people and so it is appropriate for it to be in the middle of his congregation.

Just inside the door of a Catholic church there is a small container of holy water. Worshippers dip their fingers into the water as they enter church and make the 'sign of the cross' on their bodies. The water has been blessed by a priest and symbolises new life and cleansing. The 'sign of the cross' indicates that this new life comes through the death of Jesus.

This symbol of new life is reinforced by the font which is also found just inside the door. This is the receptacle which holds the water when a baby is baptised and its position indicates the Catholic belief that baptism is the door into the fellowship of the Church. The Catholic Church has always believed that:

"There is no salvation outside the Church."

In more modern churches, however, the font is moved into the middle of the congregation. Again, this has an important symbolic significance. It is a reminder to the family of the baby, and the congregation, that baptism brings a baby into the warmth and protection of the Church fellowship, which then undertakes to cherish, love and care for it.

The High Altar

In traditional churches the high altar stands, together with a crucifix and candles, in the middle of the east wall. The east wall was originally chosen as the location for this, the most holy part of a church, because the sun rises in the east. A tabernacle (cupboard) stands behind the altar or in a side-chapel containing the 'Reserved Sacrament' (consecrated bread), which is used every time that the Mass is celebrated. The Mass is the central act of worship in every Catholic church and is celebrated every day.

At certain times of the year, most notably Lent, crucifixes are covered but they are usually visible to remind people of the sufferings and death of Jesus. Many Catholics find it very moving to pray in front of a crucifix. Often the letters INRI can be seen above the figure of Jesus, as a reminder that the figure on the cross is 'Jesus of Nazareth, King of the Jews'.

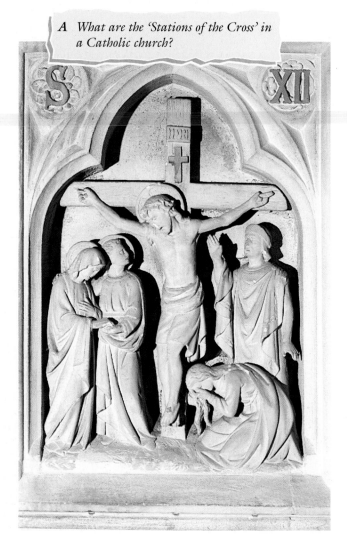

A *What are the 'Stations of the Cross' in a Catholic church?*

Around the church

On the wall of a Catholic church there are carved statues or pictures showing the 'Stations of the Cross'. These Stations are usually in stone although they can be made from other materials such as fabric, as the picture on this page shows. The Stations of the Cross illustrate the different places at which , according to the Gospels and tradition, Jesus stopped on the way to his crucifixion. Statues of the Virgin Mary

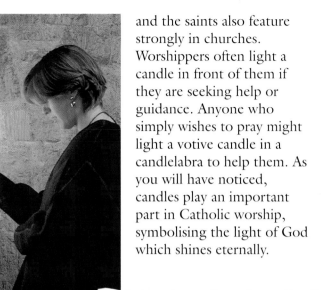

and the saints also feature strongly in churches. Worshippers often light a candle in front of them if they are seeking help or guidance. Anyone who simply wishes to pray might light a votive candle in a candlelabra to help them. As you will have noticed, candles play an important part in Catholic worship, symbolising the light of God which shines eternally.

C Can you explain the frequent link in Catholic spirituality between prayer and the lighting of candles?

B Can you find out why the altar is at the centre of worship in a Roman Catholic Church?

5.2 THE LITURGY

Worship stands at the centre of the Catholic Church's life and also that of each individual believer. Such worship can best be described as:

> "...any act of reverence or honour which is shown towards God."

Worship (worth-ship) is the giving to God of that 'which he is worth' and, as such, embraces both the formal acts of worship which take place in church and the ordinary deeds of human life which flow from a spiritual attitude of reverence for God.

Christian worship is rooted in Jesus Christ. It is Jesus alone who is able, through the Holy Spirit, to worship God in all his fullness. This is what makes Christian worship different from any other kind of religious worship. Catholic worship finds its supreme expression in the Eucharist or Mass.

The liturgy

The liturgy is the official form that Catholic worship takes. It is the public worship which the Church, as a community, offers to God through the power of the Holy Spirit. As such, it is very important since it is, in the words of the Second Vatican Council:

> "...the summit towards which the activity of the Church is directed; at the same time it is the fountain from which all power flows."
> (Constitution on the Sacred Liturgy n 10)

In other words, it is the main way by which the faithful express in their lives, and show to others, the mystery of Christ and the nature of the true Church. For this reason, every Catholic must frequently share in the sacraments and rites of the Church while giving themselves continually to prayer, self-denial and the active service of others.

What about the word itself? 'Liturgy' comes from a Greek word meaning 'a public work' and this is why Orthodox Christians speak of their equivalent of Holy Communion as the 'Divine Liturgy'. In the Catholic Church, this liturgy is set within the context of the Church Year. In a twelve monthly cycle the Church, through its worship, unfolds the whole mystery of Christ. This is expressed through the following:

a) *The Sacraments.* These are the most important acts of worship which the Church is able to offer to God. The sacraments are acts of worship offered to God by the command of Christ. They are also the very acts of worship by which Christ draws near to his people by the work of the Holy Spirit. At the centre of this sacramental worship is the Mass, which is celebrated every day.

b) *The liturgical festivals.* These festivals celebrate events in the life and death of Jesus. They culminate in the solemn, and joyful, days of Maundy Thursday, Good Friday and Easter Sunday.

c) *The great Spirit-giving event of Pentecost.* Without the work of the Holy Spirit, true worship would be impossible and without the Day of Pentecost, there would be no gift of the Spirit. Each year, therefore, Pentecost is celebrated with a real note of thanksgiving and praise.

A For many Christians a garden, and the whole of nature, have sacramental importance. What do you think is meant by this?

d) *The longed-for return of Christ to the earth.* Through its liturgy the Church looks back to what Christ accomplished by his death and resurrection; it looks through its faith at what God is doing in the world today and it looks forward to the end of time. Little wonder, then, that the Church places such importance on its liturgy.

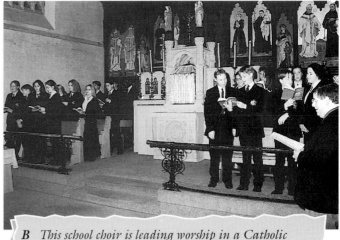

B *This school choir is leading worship in a Catholic Church. Why do you think that music has always played such an important role in the Church's liturgy?*

C *Why do you think it is important for the Catholic Church to have set liturgies?*

5.3 PRAYER (1)

The Catechism asks the question "How do we obtain God's Grace?" and answers it simply:

> "We must obtain God's grace chiefly by prayer and the holy Sacraments."

Here, and in Unit 5.4, we take an extended look at the Catholic practice of prayer. Like other aspects of Catholic spirituality, prayer has its roots in the Scriptures.

In the Scriptures

The word 'prayer' comes from the Latin word 'precari' – to entreat or to beg. Prayer is a conscious raising of the heart and mind to God, an act by which one comes into communion with God. As such, it plays a tremendously important part in the personal devotional life and public worship of most Catholics. In the Old Testament there are two main reasons for prayer:

1 To give praise to God.
2 To meet a basic human need.

Both of these ideas are carried over into the New Testament. In the Old Testament the greatest collection of prayers is the Psalms, which were written especially for worship in the great Temple in Jerusalem. They still form an essential element in most Catholic services today.

At the beginning of the ministry of Jesus we find him praying (Luke 3.21-22) whilst shortly afterwards he spent forty days praying and fasting in the desert (Luke 4.1-12). A little later we find Jesus withdrawing from the crowds to pray (Luke 5.16). The best known prayer is the Lord's Prayer (Matthew 6.9-13), which Jesus offered as a 'model prayer' to his

disciples. As such, it remains an essential ingredient in almost every act of Catholic worship.

Kinds of prayer

Different kinds of prayer may be distinguished by the purposes for which they are offered. Amongst the most important are the following:

a) *The prayer of adoration.* This offers praise and glory to God simply because of who God is. It needs no other justification.

b) *The prayer of thanksgiving.* Once a person has appreciated who God is and what he has done for them, the prayer of thanksgiving inevitably follows. The whole of the Eucharist is an extended example of this kind of prayer.

c) *The prayer of contrition.* Faced with who God is, and humbled by one's own sinfulness, the prayer of contrition must follow. This expresses a deep sorrow for all the sins one has committed and it is the prerequisite for enjoying fellowship with God.

d) *The prayer of intercession or petition.* Only when a person has appreciated the character of God and expressed their own contrition can they then pray for themselves and for others. 'Intercession' means pleading with God.

A *Do you think that prayer is a skill, something that can be learned and taught?*

B *What do you think might be the motives of this person in praying?*

All of these prayers find a prominent place in communal worship, which is nearly always liturgical. Most non-liturgical prayer is offered in the course of a person's private devotions. These devotions sometimes involve the use of a rosary and we will look at this aid to private prayer in Unit 5.4. This has long been a part of personal devotion for many older Roman Catholics.

READ AND DECIDE ...

The Lord's Prayer, or the 'Our Father', is the most familiar of all Christian prayers. Even though you are probably already familiar with it, read it through very carefully:

"Our Father, which art in heaven,
Hallowed be thy name.
Thy kingdom come,
Thy will be done,
In earth as it is in heaven.
Give us this day our daily bread,
And forgive us our trespasses
As we forgive those who have trespassed against us.
And lead us not into temptation
But deliver us from evil
For thine is the kingdom, the power and the glory,
For ever and ever.
Amen." (Matthew 6.9-13)

Can you remember the four different kinds of prayer? If the prayer of Jesus is really a model, then each of these four elements should be reflected in it.

a) Can you find the four different elements of prayer in the Lord's Prayer?

b) Can you explain how the 'Our Father' reflects that which should be present in all genuine prayer?

ANSWER IN YOUR BOOK ...

1 What is meant by 'prayer'?
2 What part did prayer play in the life of Jesus?
3 What different kinds of prayer are there?

WHAT DO YOU THINK?

a) Clearly, public and personal prayer requires a measure of faith on the person's behalf. What do you think 'faith' means in this particular context?

b) Do you think that most people pray because they have faith? Is it possible to pray if you do not have faith in the first place? Is a person's faith increased because they pray?

IN THE GLOSSARY ...

Catechism; Sacrament; Old Testament; Psalms; Lord's Prayer; Eucharist; Catholic Church; Rosary; Holy Scriptures; Fasting; New Testament.

5.4 PRAYER (2)

There are many different ways of praying. 'Mental prayer' may or may not use words. If words are used, they do not usually follow a prescribed pattern. 'Vocal prayer' does make use of a set formula of words which may be either said or sung. 'Bodily prayer' simply makes use of movement, such as dance, to express one's deepest feelings to God. Within the worship of the Catholic Church, two aspects of prayer have received particular prominence over the centuries.

Meditation and contemplation

The Catholic Church has a very strong monastic tradition which goes back to the 4th century. Both meditation and contemplation belong firmly to this tradition although, in recent years, monks and nuns have made great efforts to share their experience of prayer with others.

Let us look at meditation first. This is a form of mental prayer which involves deep concentration on the presence and activity of God. Found in other religions as well as Christianity, meditation controls the mental faculties, so that the person can focus and become aware of the presence of God.

Contemplation is a step beyond meditation. Through it a person becomes increasingly aware of the joy and beauty of God; of infinity and truth and of the majesty and love of God. In its most intense form, contemplation leads to an ecstatic union between the person and God, when he or she loses all physical contact with the world. This is sometimes called 'absorption' or 'rapture'.

The rosary

The rosary is a traditional Roman Catholic aid to prayer. It is made up of five groups of ten beads which are separated on a string from each other by single beads. These are easily distinguishable to the touch. Attached to one of these single beads is a group of three more beads, another single bead, and a cross or a crucifix.

In using a rosary four prayers are involved:

1 The prayers start at the crucifix with the Creed.
2 The 'Our Father' (see Unit 5.3) is said on the single bead.

A *This modern sculpture shows a person meditating. What are the main features of this particular form of praying?*

3 A 'Hail Mary' (Refer to **WHAT DO YOU THINK?**) is said on each of the group of three beads.
4 The 'Glory be' or 'Gloria' (Refer to **READ AND DECIDE…**) is said on the single bead which comes to the circle.

In this way, the worshipper works his or her way around the whole set of beads. While saying their prayers, the person also contemplates 15 holy 'mysteries', or events, in the life of Jesus. These are divided into three groups:

a) The 'joyful' mysteries associated with the birth and childhood of Jesus (the Annunciation, the Birth of Jesus etc).

b) The 'sorrowful' mysteries associated with the death of Jesus (the Agony in Gethsemane, the Crowning with thorns etc).

c) The 'glorious' mysteries (including the resurrection of Jesus and the taking up into heaven of the Virgin Mary).

For some Catholics who use a rosary (from the word for 'rose-garden'), the fingering of the beads is as automatic to them as is the saying of the familiar prayers. This leaves them free to meditate on the most important events in the life of Jesus. It also enables them to understand the relevance of those events for their own lives.

B Why do you think that many people find it easier to have an aid, like a rosary, in their prayers?

ANSWER IN YOUR BOOK ...

1 What is the difference between meditation and contemplation?

2 What is a rosary?

3 What are the fifteen Mysteries?

WHAT DO YOU THINK?

The 'Hail Mary' is a brief but very important prayer in Catholic devotion:

"Hail Mary (or Rejoice Mary),
Full of grace, the Lord is with thee.
Blessed art thou among women
And blessed is the fruit of thy womb, Jesus.
Holy Mary, Mother of God,
Pray for us sinners, now
and at the hour of our death,
Amen."

a) Part of the prayer reminds us of the time when the Angel Gabriel confronted Mary. Can you give an account of this occasion and explain the presence of the Angel Gabriel?

b) Who first called Mary 'blessed'? What do you think was the significance of this greeting?

c) Why do you think that Mary is addressed in this prayer as the 'Mother of God'?

d) Why do you think we need to pray to Mary 'at the hour of our death'?

READ AND DECIDE ...

The Lord's Prayer and the Hail Mary are linked with the Gloria to form a trinity of basic Catholic prayers. The Gloria is very brief:

"Glory be to the Father, and to the Son, and to the Holy Spirit. As it was in the beginning, is now and ever shall be, world without end. Amen."

a) These three prayers are often said one after the other. Can you explain the links between the three prayers?

b) How would you describe the basic idea behind the Gloria?

c) How does the Gloria embrace the whole of history?

d) How would you explain the phrase 'world without end'?

IN THE GLOSSARY ...

Catholic Church; Meditation; Contemplation; Monk; Nun; Rosary; Crucifix; Creed; Our Father; Hail Mary; Virgin Mary

5.5 THE LAITY

The 'laity' is a term used to described all those members of the Catholic Church who are neither ordained nor members of a Religious Order. These people, constituting the vast majority of the Church membership, are essential members of the Body of Christ (the Church) and have their full part to play in carrying the Gospel to the world. This was one of the basic messages underlined by the Second Vatican Council.

The Church insists that:

1 all Christians are holy because they have been possessed by the Holy Spirit;
2 all Christians are called to be active workers within the Church;
3 All Christians are called to take part in the role of Jesus Christ in the world today.

The Holy Spirit gives them the power and authority of God, just as He does to those who have been ordained. The laity are not to be thought of as mere assistants to those who are ordained – they are God's co-workers together.

The vocation of the laity

Men and women who enter the priesthood or a Religious Order need a vocation – to be certain that God has called them to the work. The laity also have a vocation or calling to serve God, wherever that might be. As Christians, they are called to share their insights, whether political, social or economic. They were reminded of this by Pope Pius XII in 1946:

> "…(the laity is) in the front line of Church life…they, in particular, ought to have an ever-clearer consciousness of belonging to the Church, that is to say, the community of the faithful on earth under the leadership of the Pope, the common Head, and of the bishops in communion with them. They are the Church."

The CCC quotes Pope Pius XII with approval. It goes on to make the following points:

a) For the true believer the whole of life – including work, prayers, married life and relaxation – can

A *What do you think is the symbolism behind a member of the congregation giving wine to others at Holy Communion?*

become spiritual sacrifices which are acceptable to God. So too, can any suffering that a person is called upon to bear. For example, parents who enjoy a married life, live in a Christian spirit and do everything to provide their children with a Christian education, are living holy lives.

b) The whole of a person's life can be offered as a sacrifice to God every time they take the Eucharist. This is the supreme sacrifice which the Church offers to God. It is also the supreme sacrifice which an individual worshipper can offer.

c) Every Church member must be constantly looking for opportunities to share the Gospel of Christ. They must also watch out for sinful activities in their own lives since these will spoil their Christian witness in the world. Having discovered the power of Christ for themselves, they must now watch for any situations in which that power can be applied:

> "...to the institutions and conditions of the world when the latter are an inducement to sin..." (CCC 909)

In other words, Catholics are in the world to change it.

B *Members of the congregation bring the offertory forward during the mass. Why do you think that the giving of money to the work of the Church is an important aspect of worship?*

d) Within the Church, each member of the laity is required to offer their God-given gifts for the benefit and blessing of the Church as a whole. As they do so they must remember a very important principle – that there is a real difference between their responsibilities to God and their responsibilities to the community around them. Having made the distinction, it is important that they carry out all their responsibilities as if they are doing them for God.

ANSWER IN YOUR BOOK ...

1 What is a vocation?

2 What does the Church mean by the 'laity' and what special role does it play in the life of the Church?

3 What is the basic characteristic of the relationship between the clergy and the laity in a church?

READ AND DECIDE ...

These words come from the CCC:
> "To teach in order to lead others to faith is the task of every preacher and of each believer... The laity can also feel called...to cooperate with their pastors in the service of the ecclesial (church) community, for the sake of its growth and life." (904/910)

In addition, the Second Vatican Council had this to say:
> "...by reason of their special vocation, it belongs to the laity to seek the Kingdom of God by engaging in temporal (earthly) affairs and directing them according to God's will...they live in the world...There they are called by God..."

a) What special vocation is given to the laity?

b) In what different ways do you think lay people might be involved in teaching within the Church?

c) How do you understand the comment that the purpose of such teaching is 'to lead others to faith...'?

d) Who are the people with whom the laity are to cooperate in the work of preaching the Gospel?

e) What is intended to be the result of all this work?

IN THE GLOSSARY ...

Laity; Catholic Church; Religious Order; Church; Gospel; Second Vatican Council; Priesthood; Vocation; Eucharist; Holy Spirit; Pope.

5.6 PILGRIMAGES

A Christian pilgrimage is a journey undertaken by believers to a place which is, for some reason, considered to be holy. No-one is under any obligation to go but religious pilgrimages have been particularly important in the Catholic Church for centuries. Many believers have seen them as an essential part of their own spiritual journey as it not only takes them to places where God, or one of his saints, have revealed themselves but it also brings them into contact with others involved on similar spiritual journeys.

Some pilgrims have their own, personal, reasons for going. Others go for the same reasons that have drawn pilgrims for centuries towards these holy places:

1 It may be their intention to say particular prayers at the shrine. As a large number of the shrines are associated with acts of healing, many pilgrims visit them seeking relief from physical or mental pain.

2 They may feel the need to thank God, the Virgin Mary or a saint for blessings that they have received in answer to prayers in the past.

3 They may want to perform an act of penance (repentance) to show their sorrow for a particular sin they have committed.

Pilgrimage centres

There are three different kinds of pilgrimage centres:

a) There are places in the Holy Land (Israel) which are visited by thousands of Christian pilgrims each year. Although pilgrims make the journey to Israel throughout the year, they particularly try to be in places associated with the birth (Bethlehem,

Nazareth) and death (Jerusalem) of Jesus at Christmas and Easter. The purpose of their pilgrimage is simple. They wish to visit the places and tread the roads which figure prominently in the Gospels. By doing so, they believe that they gain a new insight into accounts, descriptions and events recorded in the Gospels. In this way, they find that they draw themselves closer to Jesus and gain a deeper understanding of his teaching.

A *Why do you think that pilgrims travel from all over the world to listen to the Pope's Easter address?*

b) Each year thousands of pilgrims visit Rome – the 'Eternal City'. St Peter is thought to be buried in the cathedral which carries his name. This is particularly important for Roman Catholics since the Pope is believed to be his successor as the Bishop of Rome. On Easter Sunday the Pope addresses the many pilgrims in their own language in St Peter's Square. Some will then go on to visit Assisi, in Italy, since it was there that St Francis was born.

B Find out as much as you can about the history of the shrine(s) in Walsingham.

c) Pilgrims also travel to many shrines associated with healings, visions or some other special event. Lourdes, in France, has been a special place of pilgrimage ever since the middle of the 19th century when a 14 year old girl had a series of visions of the Virgin Mary. A spring of water appeared and healings have been associated with the site ever since 1873. A similar shrine is situated at Walsingham, in Norfolk. It was there, in the 11th century, that Lady Richeldis had a vision of the Virgin Mary and was told to build an exact copy of the house of Jesus in Nazareth. A well at Walsingham is credited with having the same healing properties as the one at Lourdes. The shrine in Walsingham was destroyed during the Reformation but was refounded earlier this century. It is now used by both Catholic and Anglican pilgrims who have separate shrines there. Special pilgrimages to Walsingham take place every Easter.

WHAT DO YOU THINK?

a) Pilgrims today travel in much more comfort to pilgrimage sites compared with pilgrims in the past. Do you think that this, in any way, detracts from the point of making the pilgrimage in the first place?

b) Why do you think that many Christians feel that it is important to visit the sites associated with Jesus? What do you think they might gain from making such a visit?

c) Do you think it is a pity that separate Catholic and Anglican shrines are maintained in Walsingham? Why do you think that the two Christian Churches feel that this is necessary?

d) Although thousands of sick pilgrims travel to holy sites to seek healing, very few are cured. Why do you think this is?

ANSWER IN YOUR BOOK ...

1 What is a pilgrimage? What distinguishes it from any other journey?

2 Why do people go on pilgrimages?

3 What marks out a site as holy and so worthy of a pilgrimage?

IN THE GLOSSARY ...

Virgin Mary; Saint; Shrine; Penance; Pilgrim; Christmas; Easter; Gospels; St Peter; Pope; Bishop of Rome; Easter Sunday.

5.7 DEATH

Death is the only certainty in life and constantly overshadows everything that we do. It reminds human beings that they are mortal and that life will inevitably end. Nothing human lasts for ever. Yet death does have a positive aspect. It completes all human actions and choices. Both of these aspects are reflected in the way that the Catholic Church deals with death. The teaching of the Church begins by looking beyond death. As the final article in the baptismal Creed states:

> "I believe…in the resurrection of the body and in life everlasting."

As we saw in Units 2.14 and 2.15, this bold statement tells Catholic believers that the Church offers:

a) a final reward in heaven for all those who are true believers;
b) a time of purification in purgatory for those who are not ready for heaven;
c) an eternity of punishment in hell for those who have continually turned their backs on the love which God has offered in this life.

There are two principles which underlie these beliefs about life after death:

1. There is a clear continuity between this life and the life to come. It is the love which a person shows to God and others in this life which will determine their existence in the life to come.
2. There is a radical break between this life and the life to come. In this life every believer is expected to live by a faith which is continually nurtured by the sacraments. In the life to come he or she will come face to face with God and will need nothing else.

The Hospice Movement

As someone approaches death they need help. In the past, hospitals have concentrated on the needs of the person's body and little else. The modern hospice movement, founded at the beginning of the 20th century by some Irish nuns, believes that the needs of the whole person, their relatives and friends, must be provided for as death approaches. It helps the person come to terms with their own impending death and provides support for relatives to look after their loved one while it is still possible.

The funeral service

The care of dying people is very important in the Catholic Church. They are offered the 'viaticum'

A Can you find out what it is that makes hospice care very special? Once you have carried out your research on the hospice movement, write down some notes in your book.

108

which is the sacrament for people facing death. This is a service of Holy Communion which strengthens and offers hope for those about to die.

The traditional funeral arrangements for Catholics who have died include the following:

a) *Prayers in the home.* Sometimes an all-night vigil or 'wake' is held as friends and relatives take turns to watch over the body. Often, though, the coffin is taken to the church on the night before the funeral and prayers are said for the soul of the deceased.

B It is an old Catholic tradition that prayers should be said in the dead person's home before the coffin is taken to church. Can you suggest any good reasons for this?

b) *A service in the church.* This takes place on the day of the burial and may include the Eucharist.

c) *Prayers at the graveside or in the crematorium.* The Catholic Church does not express any strong opinion over whether a person should be buried or cremated. As with Orthodox burials, in the Catholic Church much use is made in the services of incense, candles and holy water.

ANSWER IN YOUR BOOK ...

1 How is death a break with what has passed and yet, in some ways, a continuity of it?

2 What is distinctive about the Hospice Movement?

3 How does the Roman Catholic Church deal with death?

FIND OUT AND NOTE ...

a) Perhaps the most famous hospice is that run by Mother Teresa in Calcutta. Carry out some research to discover the following:
   ❖ What is the name of the order of nuns which Mother Teresa founded?
   ❖ What is the story behind the setting up of this and other hospices by Mother Teresa and her nuns?
   ❖ What was the motive behind the work carried out by this order?

b) Is there a hospice in your area? If so, find out as much as you can about it, paying particular attention to the following points:
   ❖ How did it start?
   ❖ How many patients does it take and what kind of work does it perform within the community?
   ❖ Does it have a religious foundation and, if so, what is it?
   ❖ What are the distinctive features about the kind of care that it offers?

DISCUSS AMONG YOURSELVES ...

By looking back to Units 2.14 and 2.15, you will be able to refresh your own memory about the Catholic Church's teaching on the following:

a) Heaven

b) Purgatory

c) Hell

IN THE GLOSSARY ...

Creed; Purgatory; Sacrament; Hospice; Heaven; Hell; Sacrament; Nun; Soul; Catholic Church; Viaticum; Eucharist; Orthodox Church

6.1 THE CHURCH YEAR

With worship in mind the Catholic Church divides the year into three 'seasons' or 'cycles'. Each season has at least one major festival which either commemorates a crucial event in the life of Jesus or in the history of the Church itself. The three cycles in the liturgical ('Church') year are the Christmas cycle, the Easter cycle and the Pentecost cycle

The Christmas cycle

The Church year begins at the end of November or the beginning of December with Advent. This is a period of four weeks leading up to the festival of Christmas during which Christians prepare their hearts and minds to welcome the birth of Jesus. This period of preparation has been part of the Church Year since the 6th century CE.

Christmas itself is the most widely celebrated of all Christian festivals. The name comes from the Old English 'Christes Maesse' or 'Christ's Mass'. For Christians of all denominations it is the time to celebrate the coming of Christ, God's Son, to earth. As Christians believe this to be the greatest of all gifts that God could give to humanity, Christmas is a time of great thanksgiving.

The Christmas cycle ends with the festival of Epiphany (manifestation). In Western Churches this day, January 6th, concentrates on the visit of the Magi (the Wise Men) to the infant Jesus. This was important because the Wise Men were the first non-Jews (Gentiles) to share in the Incarnation (birth) of Jesus.

The Easter Cycle

While Christmas might be the most widely celebrated Christian festival, Easter is the most important to the Church. It begins with Lent, when Catholics enter a period of reflection and preparation before Easter. The last week of Lent is 'Holy Week'. There are five important celebrations in Holy Week:

a) *Palm Sunday* – when Jesus entered Jerusalem riding on a donkey.
b) *Maundy Thursday* – when Jesus washed the feet of his disciples and ate his last meal with them.
c) *Good Friday* – which recalls the crucifixion of Jesus.
d) *Holy Saturday* – when the burial of Jesus is brought to mind.
e) *Easter Sunday* – when Christians celebrate the return of Jesus from the dead (the Resurrection). The belief that Jesus is alive is the cornerstone of the Christian faith and stands at the very heart of the Catholic faith.

The Pentecost cycle

With Easter over, one major Christian festival remains. This is the festival of Pentecost (Whitsun), when Christians celebrate the giving of the Holy Spirit to the first Christians in Jerusalem and the birthday of the Christian Church. There are also special Saints Days such as All Saints (November 1st) and All Souls Day (November 2nd).

> **A** *Find out as much as possible about the different symbols which appear in church at Christmas time.*

B *What can you find out about how Christians in your area celebrate Good Friday and Easter Sunday? In particular, are there any interesting customs or practices such as marches, sun-rise services etc?*

ANSWER IN YOUR BOOK ...

1 Into which three seasons, or cycles, does the Church divide the year?

2 What event is celebrated by Christians at Easter?

3 What important events are celebrated on Good Friday and Easter Sunday?

FIND OUT AND NOTE ...

a) Can you find out which traditions and customs are associated with the season of Advent?

b) Can you find out which 'manifestations' are still associated with the festival of Epiphany?

c) Can you find out what the significance is of Shrove Tuesday and Ash Wednesday at the beginning of Lent?

d) Can you find out which event in the life of Jesus is the model for the Christian celebration of Lent?

e) Can you find out about any special events or customs in the Catholic Church concerning Lent and Easter?

f) Can you find out how the Catholic Church celebrates Pentecost?

IN YOUR OWN WORDS ...

Conduct your own research and then write short notes on each of the following:

a) Advent

b) Christmas

c) Epiphany

d) Lent

e) Easter

f) Pentecost

IN THE GLOSSARY ...

Christmas; Epiphany; Easter; Lent; Holy Week; Palm Sunday; Maundy Thursday; Good Friday; Easter Sunday; Incarnation; Gentile; Catholic Church; Advent; Disciple; Pentecost; Whitsun; Holy Spirit.

6.2 ADVENT

The Church (liturgical) year begins with Advent. This time of preparation for the family festival of Christmas begins on the Sunday closest to November 30th and is then celebrated on the three following Sundays. It runs all the way through to Christmas Eve.

A time of preparation

For Christians of all denominations the coming of God's Son into the world was a momentous event in every sense. So momentous, in fact, that most of them set aside four weeks to prepare themselves to celebrate it. The hymns and Bible readings during Advent tell of three 'comings':

1 *The 'coming' of God's promised Messiah.* Throughout the Old Testament God led the Jews to expect that he would send them a divine leader who would deliver them from their enemies and set up the Kingdom of God on earth. The prophets, in particular, looked forward to the coming of the Messiah and readings from them, especially Isaiah, play a prominent part in church worship during Advent. Christians believe that Jesus was this long awaited figure.

2 *The 'coming' of John the Baptist.* The story of the birth of Jesus, in the Gospels of Matthew and Luke, is intertwined with the account of the birth of his cousin, John the Baptist. The birth of John was looked upon as something of a miracle since his parents, Zechariah and Elizabeth, were well past normal child-bearing age. John was important because he played a very valuable role in the early ministry of Jesus – as you can find out from Luke 1.76. (Refer to READ AND DECIDE...) By baptising the people after they had repented of their sins, John was preparing the people for the coming of Jesus.

3 *The second 'coming' of Christ to the world.* Christians believe that Christ will return to the world at the end of time to be its judge. Because this event (the Second Coming) is still awaited, it is timely that Christians should be reminded of it at Advent.

Beliefs and Advent

Two very important Christian beliefs are incorporated within the Advent celebrations. They are the following:

a) There is something very special about the birth of Jesus, the Son of God. The mother of Jesus is Mary, the Virgin, who conceived her baby by the power of the Holy Spirit and who remained a virgin during her pregnancy and the birth of Jesus. We have already looked at the 'Virgin Birth' in Unit 2.12.

A *This banner looks forward to the second coming of Christ to the world. Can you find out what Catholics believe will happen when this event takes place?*

b) That the baby who was born to Mary is the long-awaited Messiah. This belief is fundamental to the whole celebration of Christmas.

An old custom associated with Advent, the Advent Wreath, brings home to us the message of the season. Four candles are placed in an evergreen wreath and these are lit on the four Sundays of Advent. Traditionally, three of the candles are purple and the fourth is pink. The Advent wreath is a good example of the use of symbolism in Christian worship:

❖ Evergreen plants are a symbol of eternity. In this case, the eternity of God.
❖ As John reminds us in his Gospel (John 8.12), Jesus was called the 'light of the world'. The flames of the candles are symbolic, then, of Christ.
❖ The colour purple is a symbol of the periods of preparation in the Church such as Advent and Lent.

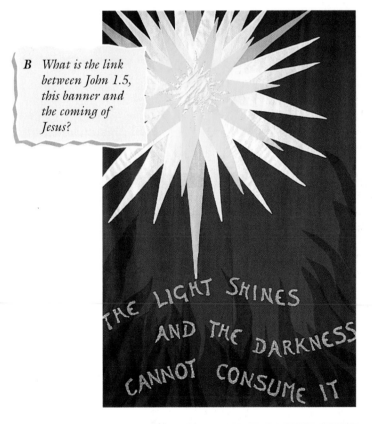

B *What is the link between John 1.5, this banner and the coming of Jesus?*

THE LIGHT SHINES AND THE DARKNESS CANNOT CONSUME IT

READ AND DECIDE ...

Here are two quotations from the New Testament. Read them carefully:

❖ "And you, little child,
you shall be called Prophet of the Most High,
for you will go before the Lord
to prepare the way for him." (Luke 1.76)

❖ "Mary, do not be afraid; you have won God's favour. Listen! You are to conceive and bear a son, and you must name him Jesus... And so the child will be holy and will be called the Son of God." (Luke 1.31,35)

a) Look up these two references and find out who is speaking on each occasion.

b) What was a prophet? What task were they expected to perform?

c) How was John the Baptist going to go 'before the Lord to prepare the way for him'?

d) What was so remarkable about the birth of Jesus?

e) What have these two quotations got to do with Advent?

CAN YOU EXPLAIN?

Can you explain the symbolism behind these Advent candles?

IN THE GLOSSARY ...

Advent; Christmas; Sunday; Old Testament; John the Baptist; Second Coming of Christ; Virgin Birth; Messiah; Kingdom of God; Prophet; Gospels; Virgin Mary; Holy Spirit; Lent.

6.3 CHRISTMAS

Although Christmas is a great family celebration, for Christians, it carries at its heart an unspeakable mystery. The Creed puts it this way:

> "I believe… in Jesus Christ, his only Son, Our Lord, who was born of the Virgin Mary."

This mystery is called the 'Incarnation' (in the flesh) and refers to the belief, held by all Christians, that God's Son, Jesus, was born as a human being in a stable in Bethlehem. It is somewhat strange, therefore, to discover that this event is only recorded by two of the four Gospels – Matthew's and Luke's. The other two Gospels, Mark and John, do not make any reference to it. For Matthew and Luke, the Incarnation emphasises two important 'truths':

1 As a human being, Jesus was the son of Mary and Joseph.
2 As a divine being, Jesus is eternally the Son of God and part of the Holy Trinity.

The humanity and the divinity of Jesus are supernaturally brought together in the Incarnation. This event is the supreme example in the Bible of God and humanity intermingling.

Celebrating Christmas

Midnight Mass on Christmas Eve is one of the best attended services of the year in most Catholic churches. Traditionally, a crib in the church depicts the traditional scene in the stable as Jesus was born. The idea of a crib is traced back to St Francis of Assisi in 1223 and this has now become a universally accepted symbol of Christmas. In most cribs the tiny figure of

A *This crib scene depicts the Incarnation. What mystery lies at the heart of this event?*

O Come Let Us Adore Him

Jesus is surrounded by his parents as well as various animals and the shepherds who, according to Luke's Gospel, came to pay their respects to him. St Francis used the crib as a visual aid for uneducated people to discover what happened at the first Christmas.

The early Christians did not celebrate the festival of Christmas. It was not until the 4th century that the date of Christmas, December 25th, was attributed to the birth of Jesus. During the reign of the first Christian Roman Emperor, Constantine, the Roman festival celebrating the birth of Mithras (the Unconquerable Sun) was Christianised and linked with the birth of Jesus. No-one is actually certain of the date on which Jesus was born.

The move towards a widespread acceptance of December 25th was led by Rome. Both the birth and baptism of Jesus were originally celebrated by Eastern churches on January 7th and some, such as the Armenian Orthodox Church, still celebrate Christmas on that date.

Epiphany and Candlemas

The Christmas season ends either with the Sunday after Epiphany or the feast of Candlemas:

a) The word 'Epiphany' means 'to show forth'. In the Gospels Jesus is 'shown forth' as the Son of God and Epiphany commemorates the following three 'showings' of Jesus:

❖ The showing of Jesus to the Wise Men, the first Gentiles to come into contact with him (Matthew 2.1-12).

❖ The Baptism of Jesus (Mark 1.9-12).

❖ The Transfiguration of Jesus (Mark 9.2-13).

b) Candlemas is the traditional day on which candles, which play such an important role in Catholic worship, were blessed. This day, February 2nd, was often known as the festival of the 'Presentation of Christ in the Temple', recalling the time when the parents of Jesus presented him to Simeon and Anna in the Temple in Jerusalem (Luke 2.25-38). Both Simeon and Anna were devout Jews who looked forward to the time when God would send his Messiah to Israel. They recognised Jesus to be that Messiah – an important belief in the early Church.

ANSWER IN YOUR BOOK ...

1 What is the 'Incarnation'?

2 Who is thought to have created the tradition of the Christmas crib? What was its original purpose?

3 What is Epiphany?

FIND OUT AND NOTE ...

Many of the traditions later associated with Christmas began as pagan or cultural traditions. What can you find out about the origins of the following customs:

a) The Christmas tree

b) Carols

c) Mistletoe

d) Yule logs

How did they come to be associated with the birth of Jesus?

READ AND DECIDE ...

The 'Song of Simeon' is found in Luke 2.29-32. Read it through carefully:
"Now, Master, you can let your servant go in peace, just as you promised;
Because my eyes have seen the salvation which you have prepared for all nations to see, a light to enlighten the pagans and the glory of your people, Israel."

Why do you think the Church has linked the festival of Candlemas with the presentation of Christ in the Temple by Simeon?

IN THE GLOSSARY ...

Creed; Christmas; Trinity; Bible; Mass; Baptism; Gentile; Incarnation; Virgin Mary; Virgin Birth; Epiphany; Gospels; Messiah.

6.4 LENT

Easter is the most important of all the Christian festivals. For this reason the Catholic Church has felt, for centuries, that a period of solemn preparation should lead up to the festival. This period of reflection, Lent, lasts for forty days. The reason for this length of time will become apparent later.

Taking Lent seriously

Lent is a time of penance and repentance – a time to prepare the body and soul for the despair and joy of Easter. It usually includes several elements:

a) *Reading the Bible and praying.* Although these two activities are regular ingredients of Catholic worship, people try to set aside more time for them during Lent.

b) *Study.* Often during Lent, Catholics come together for study-groups. Time is then spent studying a theme from the Bible.

c) *Fasting.* This may involve giving up certain types of food over the period of Lent. It may also involve trying to remedy particular defects in one's character. Self-denial has always been an important ingredient in taking Lent seriously.

d) *Good works.* Christians often increase their contributions to charities or other forms of important social work during Lent. The festival is a time for remembering the poor, the homeless and other needy people in society.

Shrove Tuesday and Ash Wednesday

Shrove Tuesday is the day before the beginning of Lent. In past centuries, people came to church on this day to make their confession and receive absolution from the priest. In the house, all of the fat was put out or used up before the fast of Lent began. In other countries this often led to a party. In Great Britain,

A Christians often use Lent to study the Bible together. Why do you think that Lent is considered to be a particularly appropriate time to do this?

however, the fat was usually used to make pancakes – a custom which is still popular today.

Ash Wednesday is the beginning of Lent and people come to church on this day to be marked on the forehead with the 'sign of the cross'. The sign is made with ash which has been made from the burning of the previous year's palm crosses. In the Old Testament, people used to put on 'sackcloth and ashes' as a sign that they were genuinely repentant for their sins. It is also a reminder that we only have a short period of time on earth. As we read in Genesis:

> "... dust you are
> and to dust you shall return". (Genesis 3.19)

Why Lent?

The length of time that Lent lasts, forty days, is significant. You may recall from the Gospel story that, after he had been baptised, Jesus went into the desert for forty days (Mark 1.12). Whilst there he fasted and prepared himself for the work that lay ahead.
By going through the ordeal of Lent Christians, too,

are preparing themselves for the task of sharing the Christian Gospel with others.

They are also spiritually preparing themselves for the events which immediately preceded the death and resurrection of Jesus. These events are celebrated within the Church as 'Holy Week'. The days of Holy Week carry a very special significance and the solemnity builds up as each day passes.

B *What do you think this worshipper is being reminded of as the priest makes the 'sign of the cross' on her forehead?*

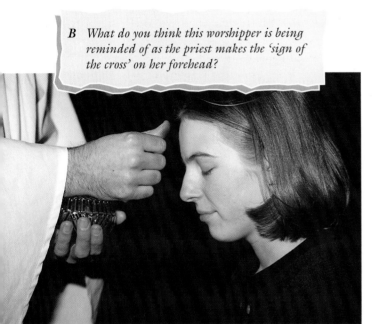

ANSWER IN YOUR BOOK ...

1 Why do Christians spend 40 days during Lent preparing themselves for Easter?

2 Why do you think that many Christians find Lent to be a spiritually valuable time?

3 What is fasting? Do you think that it could be a valuable spiritual exercise? If so, why?

WHAT DO YOU THINK?

As the priest makes the sign of the cross on the forehead of each worshipper on Ash Wednesday he says:

"Remember O man that dust thou art and to dust shalt thou return."

a) Can you explain why these words are particularly appropriate for Ash Wednesday?

b) What is the priest trying to remind the worshipper of when he says these words?

c) Why do you think that crosses from the previous Palm Sunday are burned to provide the ash for Ash Wednesday?

FIND OUT AND NOTE ...

The practice of fasting can be traced back to the Bible and the worship of the Early Church. Carry out some research to discover the following:

a) What did fasting actually involve? What did Christians give up and why did they do this? Did people regularly give up the basic necessities of life or was it confined to certain times/festivals?

b) What was the real purpose of fasting? What was the link thought to be between denying the needs of the body and obtaining spiritual blessings?

c) Why has fasting largely died out within the Christian Church as a spiritual exercise? Do you think that it can still fulfil any useful function today?

IN THE GLOSSARY ...

Easter; Lent; Fasting; Shrove Tuesday; Ash Wednesday; Old Testament; Gospel; Holy Week; Bible; Sign of the Cross.

6.5 HOLY WEEK

The last week of Lent is called 'Holy Week'. Many of the days of this week have a special relationship with highly significant events in the closing stages of Jesus's life. They are:

a) Palm or Passion Sunday
b) Maundy Thursday
c) Good Friday
d) Holy Saturday
e) Easter Sunday

Palm Sunday

At the beginning of the last week in his life Jesus entered the city of Jerusalem riding a donkey. As Matthew tells us, this took place to fulfil a prophecy from the Old Testament:

> "Say to the daughter of Zion;
> Look, your king comes to you;
> he is humble, he rides on a donkey,
> and on a colt, the foal of a beast of burden."
> (Zechariah 9.9)

This was a public statement of intent. In the peoples imagination horses were animals of war but donkeys were beasts of peace. Here was the King of Peace riding into the capital city of Israel and announcing publicly that in his kingdom:

> "The wolf lives with the lamb,
> the panther lies down with the kid,
> calf and lion eat together
> with a little boy to lead them.
> The cow and the bear make friends…"
> (Isaiah 11.6)

Christians today continue this theme on Palm Sunday as they welcome the King of Peace, Jesus. They also know that the events of Palm Sunday were soon to be overtaken by the looming shadow of the cross and this is why members of the congregation on this day are given small palm crosses. Christian services often end with a procession of the people being led out of church by a donkey in a kind of acted parable.

During the Eucharist on Palm Sunday, the long Gospel reading is taken up with the suffering and trials of Jesus. These events, known as the 'passion' of Jesus,

A *What are people being reminded of when they are given a palm cross on Palm Sunday?*

remind the people that Jesus was crucified in the same week as he entered the city of Jerusalem in triumph. Crosses and crucifixes in church are covered or removed.

On the Monday, Tuesday and Wednesday of Holy Week extra services often take place at which more passages from the Gospels are read. This is then followed by Maundy Thursday.

Maundy Thursday

Taken from the Latin word 'mandatum' –'order' – Maundy Thursday reminds us of the 'new commandment' which Jesus gave to his disciples on the day before he was crucified:

> "… love one another;
> just as I have loved you,
> you must also love one another…" (John 13.34)

Jesus said this to them after he had washed their feet. Following his example, the Pope, and other Christian leaders, have often washed the feet of the people on this day. On Maundy Thursday, Catholic priests are reminded of the solemn promise that they made at their ordination to consecrate the bread and wine for the people. They celebrate the Eucharist on Maundy Thursday with the bishop of their diocese. At the same service the bishop consecrates the oil that is going to be used in the sacraments throughout his diocese in the coming year.

On Maundy Thursday evening the Last Supper is remembered. White vestments are worn by priests and the Gloria is sung for the first time since Ash Wednesday. At the Gloria the bells are rung before falling silent until Holy Saturday. The altar is bare and empty while members of the congregation mount a vigil in a side chapel – just as the disciples were asked to do by Jesus in the Garden of Gethsemane (Mark 14.32-42).

B *What do you think is meant when this Palm Sunday procession is called an 'acted parable'?*

WHAT DO YOU THINK?

a) Which 'new commandment' did Jesus give to his disciples at the Last Supper?

b) What link does this 'new commandment' have with Maundy Thursday?

c) What is special about the Eucharist celebrated by Catholic priests on Maundy Thursday?

d) When Church leaders wash the feet of the people on Maundy Thursday what message do you think they are sending? How does this tie in with what you read in John 13.12-15?

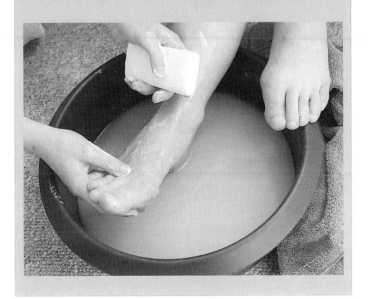

ANSWER IN YOUR BOOK ...

1 What is Holy Week?

2 Why did Jesus enter Jerusalem on a donkey? How do many Christians re-enact this event today?

3 How do Christians remind themselves of the link between the events of Palm Sunday and the death of Jesus?

FIND OUT AND NOTE ...

Carry out some research of your own before writing up notes on each of the following:

a) The entry of Jesus into the city of Jerusalem on a donkey (Luke 19.28-44).

b) Celebrating Palm Sunday.

c) Jesus washing the feet of his disciples (John 13.1-17).

d) Celebrating Maundy Thursday.

IN THE GLOSSARY ...

Lent; Gospels; Bishop; Diocese; Altar; Holy Week; Palm Sunday; Maundy Thursday; Good Friday; Easter Sunday; Old Testament; Eucharist; Pope; Priest; Sacrament; Last Supper; Ash Wednesday.

6.6 GOOD FRIDAY

For Christians from all denominations, Good Friday is the most solemn day of the year. On this day, their thoughts turn to the brutal death of Jesus on Calvary at the hands of the Roman soldiers. Often, the shared grief that Christians feel as they remember the death of Jesus on this day draws them together across denominational barriers. They take part in processions throughout their locality which re-enact the last few hours in the life of Jesus on his way to the cross. For those taking part this provides a two-fold opportunity:

1 It gives them the opportunity to meditate upon the shame and agony which accompanied the death of Jesus.
2 It provides a witness to the whole community that Jesus died for the whole world. On this belief all Christians can agree.

This testimony to the community begins to explain why this day is strangely called 'Good' Friday. It was the 'goodness' of Jesus which compelled him to die on the cross.

Good Friday in church

On Good Friday, church services traditionally start at three o'clock in the afternoon – the time when the Gospels tell us that Jesus died. This service provides an opportunity for worshippers to meditate on the last few hours in the life of Jesus through prayers and readings from one of the Gospels – usually that of John. Two distinctive events also take place during those Good Friday services which are held in a Catholic church:

a) Members of the congregation visit the fourteen 'Stations of the Cross' which are situated around the inside or outside walls of the church and pray in front of them. These statues or pictures represent those places where, according to the Holy Scriptures and tradition, Jesus stopped or stumbled on his way to Calvary. The people in church become 'pilgrims' just as those who, at the very same time, are walking up the 'Via Dolorosa' in Jerusalem. The pilgrims in church make their way from one picture to another, kneeling at each scene and reciting appropriate prayers. This act of devotion is at the heart of the Good Friday service. Through it worshippers are sharing, in a small way, in the sufferings of Jesus.

b) In a part of the service called 'The Veneration of the Cross', a veiled crucifix is taken to a place in the middle of the church and gradually uncovered before the people. Everyone, priest and people alike, kiss it to show their respect and love for Jesus, who was crucified two thousand years ago.

So Good Friday ends. The grief of the day, however, is tempered by the knowledge that Christians will shortly be sharing in the happiness and pleasure of Easter Sunday.

Holy Saturday

Within the Orthodox and Catholic churches the day between Good Friday and Easter Sunday is a time of quiet anticipation. Churches are thoroughly cleaned and the best altar-linen and vessels are brought out and arranged for Easter Day. During the day, Christians remember what it cost Jesus to pay the price for their

sins. His suffering, though, is now over. On this day, according to the Gospel story, his body lay in a borrowed tomb. On Easter Day, Christians will be celebrating the new life associated with Jesus rising from the dead.

ANSWER IN YOUR BOOK ...

1 Why do Catholics come together to worship and meditate at three o'clock on Good Friday afternoon?

2 What are the main features of Good Friday services in a Catholic church?

3 What happens during the 'Veneration of the Cross'? Why do you think this is an important act of Catholic devotion?

WHAT DO YOU THINK?

a) Why do you think that it is especially important for churches of all denominations to show their unity on Good Friday – of all days in the Church year?

b) Good Friday is used by most Christians as a day for meditation. On what do they meditate and why do you think this spiritual exercise is particularly appropriate on this day?

c) Why do you think that worshippers in a Catholic church, and pilgrims in the Holy Land, visit the different 'Stations of the Cross' on Good Friday? What might they hope to gain from doing this?

d) Why do you think that Catholic churches make a point of using the best altar-cloths and vessels on Easter Sunday?

A *Can you explain why these Christians are taking part in this open display of their faith on Good Friday?*

CAN YOU EXPLAIN?

In these photographs you can see two 'Stations of the Cross'.

a) What are the Stations of the Cross and why do they play an important part in Catholic worship on Good Friday?

b) Can you explain what is happening in the two Stations shown in the photographs?

c) Can you find out what the other Stations of the Cross are? Which of them illustrate 'events' that are not mentioned in the Gospel accounts of the death of Jesus?

IN THE GLOSSARY ...

Good Friday; Gospels; Stations of the Cross; Holy Scriptures; Priest; Holy Saturday; Orthodox Church; Catholic Church; Easter Sunday; Crucifix.

6.7 EASTER SUNDAY

On Easter Sunday, the most joyful and important day in the whole Church year, Christians celebrate the resurrection of Jesus from the dead. This belief, more than any other, is the foundation upon which the whole Christian faith is built. It is somewhat strange to find, therefore, that the festival which commemorates this great event, like the festival of Christmas, began life as a pagan festival. The word 'Easter' itself comes from the Anglo-Saxon 'Eostre', referring to the goddess of Spring. In the 2nd century it was usual to hold an Easter vigil on the night that Christ 'passed over' from death to life and this custom is still continued in the Orthodox and Catholic Churches. It is from this that the festival of Easter started.

Easter Day in church

Most churches are decorated with flowers on Easter Day as a symbol of the new life of Christ. In Catholic churches the celebrations begin as it grows dark on the Saturday. The Paschal Candle ('the candle of suffering') is then lit and carried into the darkened church, symbolising the light that has been brought into the world through Christ's resurrection from the dead. The worshippers light their own candles from the Paschal Candle until the whole church is glowing with light.

Apart from the obvious symbol of light that the Paschal Candle

represents, it also contains two Greek letters – Chi and Rho. These are the first two letters of the name 'Christ'. Five grains of incense are placed in the centre of the candle to commemorate the five wounds of Christ. The candle has the year printed on it and the first and last letters of the Greek alphabet – Alpha and Omega.

On Easter Day the clergy wear their brightest vestments for Mass. Church bells are rung for the first time since Good Friday and the service opens with a rousing resurrection hymn. The readings tell the story of the resurrection and the homily draws attention to the 'new life' which everyone receives through the resurrection of Jesus. Worshippers often join in the ancient response:

"The Lord is risen! He is risen indeed!"

During the Mass three important events – the death of Jesus, the resurrection of Christ and the return of Jesus to the earth in glory – are linked together in the words:

"Dying you destroyed our death, rising you restored our life. Lord Jesus, come in glory."

With these words the Church sums up the Easter faith. It is the faith which forms the core of the Gospel to which the Catholic Church is so totally committed.

A Why do you think that the symbol of light dispelling darkness is so powerful on Easter Sunday?

The Easter Faith

The Easter Faith stands at the very centre of the Catholic Church's belief and worship. As the CCC states:

> "The Resurrection of Jesus is the crowning truth of our faith in Christ, a faith believed and lived as the central truth by the first Christian community..." (638)

Christians believe that Christ rose from the dead on the third day after he was crucified. The Gospels do not agree on the details of what happened. All of them, though, bear witness to the belief of the early Christians that the tomb was empty when the women went to anoint the body of Jesus early on the first Easter Day. Jesus had been raised by the power of God from the grave. This belief has been the cornerstone on which the faith of the Catholic Church has been built ever since.

B *If you were asked to sum up, in just one sentence, the essential message of Easter for the Christian Church, what would you say?*

ANSWER IN YOUR BOOK ...

1 What was the origin of the word 'Easter'?
2 What is distinctive about Easter Sunday services in the Catholic Church?
3 What essential message is preached on Easter Sunday?

CAN YOU EXPLAIN?

a) Can you explain why the Paschal Candle is an important Easter symbol?
b) Can you explain why the Paschal Candle is carried into a darkened church for the whole congregation to light their own candles from?
c) Somewhere on each Paschal Candle you will find the Greek letters Alpha and Omega. You can find out why these particular letters are used by looking up Revelation 22.13. Try to explain it in your book.

IN YOUR OWN WORDS ...

The CCC summarizes the teaching of the Church on the resurrection of Jesus by quoting words from an old liturgy:

> "Christ has risen from the dead
> By his death he has vanquished death
> To the dead he has given life." (638)

Describe the following in your own words:

a) Just what the Catholic Church believes about the resurrection of Jesus from the dead?
b) Just why the Catholic Church believes that the resurrection of Jesus is so important?

IN THE GLOSSARY ...

Easter Sunday; Christmas; Orthodox Church; Catholic Church; Paschal Candle; Mass; Good Friday; Gospels.

6.8 ASCENSION DAY AND PENTECOST

Easter brings to a close the two main cycles in the Church year. There are still some important festivals to come, and these centre around Pentecost (Whitsun), which commemorates the occasion when the Holy Spirit was given to the first Christian disciples in Jerusalem (Acts 2.1-8).

Before Pentecost, however, comes Ascension Day.

Ascension Day

Ascension Day always comes forty days after Easter and so falls each year on a Thursday. It marks the occasion, recorded in Mark 16.19, 20 and Acts 1.6-11, when Jesus left his disciples for the last time and returned to his Father in heaven. Before he left them, however, Jesus told them to go out into the world and preach the Gospel.

Ascension Day is a Holy Day (a Day of Obligation) in the Catholic Church and a Mass is always celebrated. The occasion is also used to encourage Christians to wait another 10 days before celebrating the giving of the Holy Spirit at Pentecost.

Pentecost

Fifty days after Easter the Church celebrates Pentecost and the coming of the Holy Spirit to the disciples in Jerusalem. This event initiated a period of intense activity among the early Christians and, according to the Acts of the Apostles, three thousand people were converted to Christ on the first day alone. The fear that the early Christians had of being handed over to the Roman authorities was gone for ever.

This festival, the birthday of the Christian Church, has two names:

a) *Pentecost*. This was derived from the name of the old Jewish harvest festival (the Feast of Weeks), with the word itself meaning 'fifty'.

b) *Whitsun*. Derived from 'White Sunday' this name was given to the festival because it was the traditional time for new converts to the Christian faith to be baptised. For this ceremony they wore white clothes as a symbol of their new-found faith in Christ. In some churches this custom is continued as confirmation services are held. During the service, the bishop lays his hands on the head of the person being confirmed and prays for the Holy Spirit to come into his or her life.

In the past, many Catholics took part in walks of witness (Whit Walks) over this weekend to symbolise the desire of the early Christians, after Pentecost, to share their faith with everyone. Now, though, worship on this day is concentrated on church. The services are held to celebrate and explain the first giving of the Holy Spirit. The clergy wear red vestments to symbolise the colour of the flames that descended on the first disciples.

A Read the story of the ascension of Christ into heaven for yourself in Acts 1.6-11. Is this how you would visualise the event?

Understanding Pentecost

During the time that Christ was on earth individuals responded to him, and his message, personally. James and John, for example, were in their boat when Jesus called them while Matthew was working as a tax-gatherer. With the giving of the Holy Spirit at Pentecost, the nature of that call changed. The focus had shifted from the individual to the community. As one Roman Catholic document states:

> "God has willed to make human beings holy and save them not as individuals, without any bond or link between them, but as people."
> (Lumen Gentium)

After Pentecost there were two stages to being accepted as a member of the Christian Church. This is illustrated by the following quotation:

> "You must repent, Peter answered, and every one of you must be baptised in the name of Jesus Christ for the forgiveness of your sins and you will receive the gift of the Holy Spirit." (Acts 2.38)

This process of repentance and baptism is continued in the Church today through the sacraments of baptism and confirmation.

READ AND DECIDE ...

a) The most common symbol of the Holy Spirit in the Church today is that of a dove. Read the following passages to work out why this is.

Genesis 8.8
❖ What does the dove represent as it is sent out to discover whether the waters of the flood have receded?

Matthew 3.16
❖ Why do you think that the Holy Spirit descends on Jesus in the form of a dove?

Matthew 10.16
❖ What characteristic of doves is highlighted here? Can you suggest why this is?

b) Strangely, this symbol does not appear in Luke's account in Acts 2.1-12. What symbols are used here for the Holy Spirit and what do you think they symbolise?

IN YOUR OWN WORDS ...

In your own words, write a paragraph comparing the story of the coming of the Holy Spirit in John 20.19-23 with Acts 2.1-8.

ANSWER IN YOUR BOOK ...

1 What event is celebrated by the Church on Ascension Day?

2 What is the significance of the names 'Whitsun' and 'Pentecost'?

3 What is distinctive about services held in church on Pentecost?

IN THE GLOSSARY ...

Gospel; Catholic Church; Day of Obligation; Disciple; Acts of the Apostles; Confirmation; Sacrament; Baptism; Bishop; Clergy; Easter Sunday; Pentecost; Whitsun; Holy Spirit; Easter; Ascension Day; Mass.

6.9 ALL SAINTS DAY AND ALL SOULS DAY

These two festivals follow one another on November 1st and 2nd. The first, All Saints Day, is a Catholic holy day of obligation.

All Saints Day

On All Saints Day the Catholic community honours all those saints who are now enjoying life with God in heaven, especially those saints who do not have 'feast days' of their own in the Church year. The word 'saint' is derived from Latin and means 'holy' or 'consecrated to God'.

From the 4th century the Catholic Church was setting aside a particular day (May 13th) to remember all Christian martyrs (those who had laid down their lives for the Christian Gospel). In the 8th century this day of celebration was changed to November and in the 12th century it officially became 'All Saints Day'. For a long time a night of prayer, waiting for a feast (a vigil) and an eight day period of prayer, after a feast, were celebrated but these are no longer part of the celebrations.

For Roman Catholics, three themes emerge from the day's celebrations:

a) It gives church members an annual opportunity to venerate all the saints of the past.
b) It provides an opportunity for all Catholics to pray for assistance with problems and difficulties.
c) It allows people today to learn how to live a life of witness and service by following the example of the saints of old.

All Souls Day

Following a day spent remembering the saints of the past who are with God in heaven, the following day, All Souls Day, is appropriate to remember the souls who are, at the present time, in purgatory. Purgatory is the spiritual state into which the souls of people who have died enter to be purified before they can go to heaven. This particular feast goes back to the 10th century. St Odilo wanted to provide the monks in his monastery with the opportunity to offer prayers and hymns for the dead on the day after All Saints Day. The practice soon became popular and spread to many church communities in Europe and Latin America.

From the 1920s, the practice developed to offering three Masses on this day. The Masses were for the following:

1 A special intention
2 The dead in purgatory
3 The Pope's intentions

Some priests still say three Masses on this day but most people believe that the number increased because of the fears and superstitions of the people about purgatory.

The keeping of All Souls Day allows for the following:

a) A reminder to Catholics that, even though some people have died and passed into the painful spiritual condition of purgatory, they will find the basic experience one of happiness. They know that they will eventually be admitted into heaven and God's presence.

A What do you think the saints from the past might be able to teach Catholics in the modern world?

b) The prayers of the people helping the souls in purgatory to overcome their spiritual separation from God.

c) Catholics spending the day doing 'works of charity' – although these should be an everyday feature for the committed Catholic.

B *Do you agree that most Roman Catholics have a deep fear of purgatory? Carry out a small survey to discover what people think.*

ANSWER IN YOUR BOOK ...

1 Can you explain what the word 'saint' means?
2 What is important to Roman Catholics about All Saints Day?
3 What does keeping All Souls Day encourage Roman Catholics to do?

IN YOUR OWN WORDS ...

Try to find out as much information as possible about each of the following and then write up a description of them in your own words:

a) A holy day of obligation
b) Venerating the saints
c) Purgatory
d) Intentions
e) Heaven
f) Works of charity

WRITE AN ESSAY ...

Write an essay of about 500 words on each of the following:

a) All Saints Day
b) All Souls Day

IN THE GLOSSARY ...

Saint; Heaven, Catholic Church; Purgatory; Mass.

6.10 SUNDAY

Each of the festivals covered in this unit so far have been celebrated annually. Sunday is different. Celebrated each week, it is still a festival since it is a time of celebration to commemorate the most important of all events – the resurrection of Jesus.

The Sabbath Day

The custom of celebrating the Sabbath Day goes all the way back to the earliest times of the Jewish people. As Jews were reminded in the Ten Commandments:

> "Remember the Sabbath Day to keep it holy." (Exodus 20.8)

It was to be a day of holiness, set aside for God, and a day of rest. It was linked with two events in Jewish history:

1 The day of divine rest which followed the six days that God had spent creating the world (Exodus 20.11).
2 The deliverance by God of the Jews from over 400 years of slavery in Egypt (Deuteronomy 5.15).

As the first Christians were almost all Jews it was natural for them to continue observing the Sabbath Day. It was only when they were prevented from worshipping in the synagogues that they began to meet together on the 'Lord's Day' – the first day of the week.

The Lord's Day

Jesus rose from the dead 'on the first day of the week' (Matthew 28.1) – the day after the Jewish Sabbath Day. By the end of the 1st century, Christians had adopted this day, the 'Lord's Day', as the most

appropriate time for their worship. As St Justin wrote midway through the 2nd century:

> "We all gather on the day of the sun, for it is the first day when God, separating matter from darkness, made the world; and on this same day Jesus Christ our Saviour rose from the dead."

According to the CCC, there are two reasons why every Catholic should feel under a strong obligation to meet with other Catholics on Sundays:

a) Sunday is the day on which the Eucharist is celebrated. This celebration is at the heart of the Church's, and each individual Catholic's, life. This makes Sunday:

> "... the foremost holy day of obligation in the universal Church..." (2192)

The Eucharist is so important that each individual believer must make every attempt to be part of its celebration week by week. St John Chrysostom pointed out back in the 5th century that it is perfectly possible to worship God in the home, but it is only in church that there is:

> "... the union of minds, the accord of souls, the bond of charity, the prayers of priests."

A *Apart from the need to worship God, can you think of anything else that a Catholic might gain from attending church regularly?*

Sunday is the supreme 'day of obligation' – although this obligation can be discharged by attending Mass on a Saturday evening if that is preferred.

b) Sunday is a day of grace and rest from work. Human life is caught up in a rhythm of work and relaxation. The Lord's Day helps everyone to enjoy adequate rest and leisure-time and is a benefit to a person's family, religious and social life. On this day, therefore, everyone should rest from any work or activity which hinders their worship of God. As the CCC states:

> "Sunday is a time for reflection, silence, cultivation of the mind and meditation which furthers the growth of the Christian interior life." (2186)

The Catholic Church feel that Sunday is so important for the well-being of each man, woman and child that the Church, wherever it is, should seek to gain recognition for Sunday and the other Church holy days as holidays to be enjoyed by all.

ANSWER IN YOUR BOOK …

1 What is the Sabbath Day?

2 Why was it natural for the early Christians to continue worshipping God on the Sabbath Day?

3 Why should a Catholic make every effort to worship God in church every Sunday?

FIND OUT AND NOTE …

The Codex Iuris Canonici, published in 1983, had this to say about Sunday:

> "Sunday… is to be observed as the foremost holy day of obligation in the universal Church".

Carry out some research to discover the following:

a) What is a 'day of obligation' and why is it important?

b) Apart from Sunday there are ten other 'days of obligation'. Can you find out what they are?

c) What are Catholics expected to do on 'days of obligation'? What do they commit if they fail?

CAN YOU EXPLAIN?

a) Can you explain why the Christian Church eventually chose to set aside Sunday as its special day of worship?

b) Can you explain why the Catholic Church places such a heavy emphasis on the importance of going to church on Sundays?

c) Can you explain just what it is that Catholics lose if they do not meet regularly with other Christians?

IN THE GLOSSARY …

Sunday; Sabbath Day; Ten Commandments; Synagogue; Eucharist; Day of Obligation.

7.1 THE FAMILY

The family is the most important unit in our society. The first people that we come to know are our parents while our brothers and sisters are our first friends. With this in mind, the CCC refers to the family as the 'domestic church', since it is within the family that Catholics have their first experiences of a Christian community. Jesus learned this with Mary and Joseph, his parents, as part of the Holy Family.

The CCC calls the family 'an original cell of social life' (2207), since people are bound to it both by nature and by blood. Through it each individual learns:

a) how to accept and exercise authority;
b) how to enjoy real freedom and yet feel secure;
c) how to accept and give both love and friendship.

Society needs a strong family structure and must do everything it can to strengthen and uphold family life. Its very future depends on it. In particular, society should maintain the right of every family to do the following:

1 Bring up its children according to the religious convictions of the parents.
2 Buy and maintain private property.
3 Have a reliable income through the hard work of its members.
4 Travel freely and live in the place of its choice.
5 Be protected against those influences which can destroy family life such as drug-taking, alcoholism and pornography.

Responsibilities

Within every family parents have responsibilities towards their children and vice versa. The CCC points these out:

a) *Childrens responsibilities towards their parents.* From the Ten Commandments we find that the first responsibility of all human beings is to love God (Exodus 20.1-11). Our next duty is to honour our parents (Exodus 20.12). We should do this out of sheer gratitude and this encourages us to be obedient to our parents – since only then can we grow in wisdom and grace. We should never stop respecting our

A *What do you think are the most important responsibilities which these parents have to their children?*

parents. Even those who have reached 'the age of majority' (adulthood) should continue to care for their parents – especially when they reach old age. Christians should show particular respect and care for those who have handed their religious faith on to them and encouraged it to grow. The same respect should be extended in other directions as well. These include the duties of pupils to teachers, employees to employers, subordinates to leaders, citizens to their country and those given the responsibility of leading it.

b) *Parents responsibilities towards their children*. The duty of parents to their children covers the whole area of physical, moral and spiritual care. As they are 'the first heralds of faith', so they are the ministers of faith for their children. Their duty is to help their children grow in virtue and holiness – a task which is helped immeasurably if their children attend a 'truly Christian school'. This will help a child to make two of the greatest decisions in life:
* the choice of taking up a particular profession and raising a family.

* the choice of responding to a religious vocation, to the priesthood or a Religious Order, and taking on the responsibility of celibacy.

B What does the Catholic Church teach about the responsibilities of these children towards their parents?

ANSWER IN YOUR BOOK ...

1 What is the 'domestic Church'?

2 What duties do parents have towards their children?

3 What are the responsibilities of children towards their parents?

READ AND DECIDE ...

Here are two quotations from the New Testament which highlight the responsibilities which children have to older members of their family. Try to work out the implications of each of them in practice:

a) "Children, be obedient to your parents always, because that is what will please the Lord." (Colossians 3.20)
* What does the word 'obedient' mean? Does this obligation towards one's parents ever end?

b) "Then I am reminded of the sincere faith which you have: it came first to live in your grandmother Lois, and your mother Eunice, and I have no doubt it is the same faith in you as well." (2. Tim 1.5)
* How difficult is it for parents to pass on their religious faith to their children? How do you think they might set about trying to do so?

WHAT DO YOU THINK?

a) What do you think the CCC means when it calls the family:
* a 'mini-church'?
* a 'mini-society'?
* the 'domestic church'?

b) What do you think the CCC means when it calls parents the 'first heralds of faith'?

c) What do you think a 'truly Christian school' is? How might this school help a child grow in holiness?

IN THE GLOSSARY ...

Ten Commandments; Vocation; Priesthood; Celibacy; Religious Order.

7.2 MARRIAGE (1)

The opening chapters of the Bible introduce us to the divine purpose and plan for marriage. Once God has created the universe, and all non-human forms of life, he creates 'man' (Genesis 1.26). Man is given the task of naming "all the wild beasts and all the birds of heaven" but is unable to find a 'helpmate' (soulmate) from amongst them. To solve this problem God makes 'woman' from a part of man's body – one of his ribs. Man is delighted with the result:

> "This at last is bone of my bones,
> and flesh from my flesh!
> This is to be called woman,
> for this was taken from man." (Genesis 2.23)

The writer then adds the significant comment:

> "This is why a man leaves his father and mother and joins himself to his wife, and they become one body." (Genesis 2.24)

The implication is that 'marriage' has been with the human race from the beginning. The phrase that the man and woman leave their respective families and together become 'one body' includes two important ideas about marriage:

1 Sexual union is basic to a marriage.
2 Through marriage two people become a single living, thinking and feeling unit.

This single unit is then given its basic task:

> "Be fruitful, multiply, fill the earth and conquer it." (Genesis 1.28)

A What do you think that a husband and wife might hope to gain from their relationship with both each other and their children?

The Catholic Church recognises this and stresses the Biblical message that the 'procreation of children' is one of the most important reasons for a man and a woman marrying. From the moment that Jesus blessed marriage by performing his first miracle at a wedding feast (John 2.1-11) he sought to uphold its dignity and permanence. The Church places great store on this miracle and sees in it a great confirmation of the goodness of marriage. Jesus would not have attended the wedding if he had not believed in its inherent goodness. He underlined this by taking a strong stand against divorce (Matthew 19.3-12). We will discover more about this in Unit 7.4.

Problems within marriage

Marriage is a vocation – a calling from God. It is part of the very nature of men and women. It is not simply a human institution. Its very origin belongs to the plan of God. God made the love between a man and a woman an image (picture) of the love that he has for the human race. Paul likened marriage to the devotion of Christ to his Church when he gave himself for it (Ephesians 5.25-31).

Yet, as everyone knows, there are deep internal problems in many marriages. Often, these problems lead to the breakdown of the marriage. This does not mean, however, that there is anything wrong with the institution of marriage. Rather, such problems reflect the basic sinfulness of human nature and can only be conquered with God's help.

Mixed marriages

Mixed marriages take place when a Catholic marries a non-Catholic. They can take one of two forms:

a) *Marriages between a Catholic and a baptised non-Catholic.* This should not present an insurmountable obstacle to marriage. They must, however, learn to share with each other what they have in common from their different backgrounds. A problem could be caused by the fact that the same differences which separate Churches might be reflected in the marriage. The couple might also disagree over such issues as family planning, abortion etc. The problems are likely to be most acute over the issue of bringing up the children. The Catholic Church insists that any offspring of a mixed marriage should be brought up as Catholics.

b) *Marriages between a Catholic and a member of another religious faith.* This is likely to be more problematical. For the marriage to take place at all a special dispensation is required from the Church. It is a great joy for the Church and for the believing spouse if their union should lead to the conversion of the other person to the Christian faith.

> **B** One of these people is a Catholic and the other belongs to the Church of England. What does the Catholic Church teach about such a "mixed marriage"?

DISCUSS AMONG YOURSELVES ...

a) What do you understand from the command of God to the first man and woman to "Be fruitful, multiply, fill the earth and conquer it. Be masters of the earth…"? (Genesis 1.28)

b) What do you understand from the statement of Jesus that as a man and a woman leave their parents and marry "so they are no longer two, but one flesh"? (Matthew 19.6)

c) What do you understand from the statement in the CCC that "Without his (God's) help, man and woman cannot achieve the union of their lives for which God created them in the beginning"? (1608)

d) What do you understand from the comment by Paul that "… the unbelieving husband is consecrated through his wife and the unbelieving wife is consecrated through her husband"? (1.Corinthians 7.14)

ANSWER IN YOUR BOOK ...

1 Where did the Christian belief about marriage originate from?

2 What explanation does the Catholic Church offer for problems within a marriage?

3 What is a 'mixed marriage'? What are the main problems they can cause?

IN THE GLOSSARY ...

Sacrament; Vocation; Original Sin; St Paul; Catholic Church; Abortion.

7.3 MARRIAGE (2)

When a couple marry in a Catholic church their union is blessed and sealed by God. God establishes their 'marriage bond' in such a way that the relationship between two baptised Catholics is permanent. The married love (conjugal love) which grows between them involves a total commitment in which bodies, feelings, minds and spirits are all present in the relationship. For this marriage to be complete three characteristics are required: indissolubility; faithfulness and an openness to fertility.

Indissolubility

The Catholic Church, following the teaching of the New Testament and its own understanding of marriage as a sacrament, is adamant that a marriage should never be dissolved. Each couple who pass through a marriage ceremony are called by God to be part of a relationship which will continue to grow throughout their lives together. The Church, through its common faith and the sacrament of the Eucharist, provides the means by which this can happen.

Christ recognised that this unity of purpose between husband and wife could only grow in a relationship in which both are given equal respect. That is why 'monogamy' (the marriage of one man to one woman) is the only relationship which receives the blessing of the Church. Both 'polygamy' (one man and several wives) and 'polyandry' (one wife and several husbands) continue to be condemned in the CCC – as they have been by the Church for centuries. This is because true love between a husband and a wife can only thrive in a relationship which is undivided and exclusive.

A *What characteristics do you think should be present to make this a truly happy and successful marriage?*

Faithfulness (fidelity)

By its very nature, conjugal love requires that a couple must be absolutely faithful to each other. This is a direct consequence of the vows that the couple made to each other, and in the sight of God, when they married. The happiness of the couple and the welfare of their children depends upon this faithfulness.

This requirement is not at all surprising. After all, the closest parallel to the relationship between Christ and the Church is the relationship between a husband and wife. Just as Christ expects total faithfulness from the body of believers, a husband and wife have the right to expect the same from each other. If a couple find this hard they must realise that they share in God's love and that this will support and sustain them in their love for each other.

An openness to fertility

This can be a problem in a mixed marriage where someone from another Christian tradition may have a very different attitude to birth-control. As we shall discover in Unit 7.8, the Catholic Church is totally opposed to any artificial forms of birth-control. To use them is to reject the natural and God-given purpose of marriage – to have the children which are a marriage's 'crowning glory'. By always keeping their marriage open to the possibility of creating new life a couple are sharing with God in the work of creation.

Children are God's supreme gift to a marriage and they bring much happiness to a husband and wife. This happiness is increased considerably if parents see their children brought up within the Catholic faith and, in turn, pass that faith on to their own children. Each Catholic family, then, must always be open to the possibility of new life.

There are, of course, many couples who are not blessed with children because either the husband or the wife is infertile. The CCC makes the following statement about these people:

"… (they can) have a conjugal life full of meaning, in both human and Christian terms. Their marriage can radiate a fruitfulness of charity, of hospitality and of sacrifice." (1654)

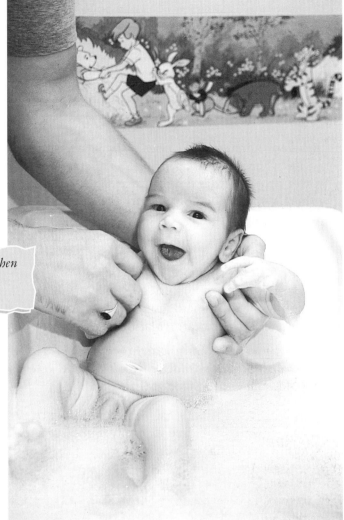

B *What do you think the Church means when it refers to children in a marriage as its 'crowning glory'?*

ANSWER IN YOUR BOOK …

1 What is monogamy and why is it essential to any marriage which is going to enjoy God's blessing?

2 What is a mixed-marriage and what problems can it present?

3 Why are children described as the 'crowning glory' of any marriage?

FIND OUT AND NOTE …

The best way to find out about marriage is to interview a Catholic couple who are prepared to answer your questions openly. Ask them the following questions:

a) Did they feel prepared for marriage when they took their vows? If not, would they have liked more help? From whom? – The Church? Their parents? Outside agencies?

b) To what extent did they find their Catholic faith helpful in their married life.

c) Has their religious faith caused any problems in their married life?

d) What do they understand when the Catholic Church refers to marriage as a sacrament?

e) Do they fully accept the Church's teaching on such matters as birth-control?

Also, feel free to ask any other questions that you think might be helpful!

CAN YOU EXPLAIN?

Can you explain why each of the following is essential in a successful marriage:

a) Indissolubility

b) Faithfulness

c) An openness to new life

IN THE GLOSSARY …

New Testament; Eucharist; Sacrament; Birth-control; Catholic Church.

7.4 DIVORCE

According to the CCC there are two 'offences' against the dignity of marriage:

1 *Adultery*. Adultery is a serious sin against God. It occurs when a married person has sexual intercourse with a person who is not their marriage partner. Adultery was condemned in both the Old and New Testaments:

- ❖ The prophets in the Old Testament put adultery on the same level as idolatry (Hosea 2.7; Jeremiah 5.7).
- ❖ Christ went even further and condemned not only adultery but also lustful thoughts as 'adultery of the heart' (Matthew 5.27,28).

Adultery is a crime against the rights of a person's partner to have that undivided love which they were promised in the sight of God at their wedding.

2 *Divorce*. Divorce is the legal break-up of a marriage leaving either partner free to legally re-marry. The Roman Catholic Church does not recognise divorce for the following reasons:

a) Christ insisted that the original intention for marriage in the plan of the Creator was that it should be indissoluble (Matthew 5.31-32; 19.3-9; Mark 10.9). Jesus even removed the acceptance of divorce which had become a part of the Jewish understanding of marriage (Matthew 19.7-9). As a Catholic document of 1983 states:

"A ratified and consummated marriage cannot be dissolved by any human power or for any reason other than death" (Codex Iuris Canonici)

b) Divorce is a grave offence against natural law. It breaks the contract that the two people made, in the sight of God, to live with each other until death parted them. If either person re-marries they live in public and permanent adultery. Moreover, the person married to a divorced person also commits adultery.

> How children are damaged by divorce
>
> Camilla parts from husband
>
> Royal divorce will go ahead, says courtier
>
> Breakdown rate Divorce help
>
> Couples get period to reflect on divorce
>
> £50m divorce deal
>
> Mediation could save marriages, claims Mackay
>
> Law and church welcome end to quickie divorces
>
> C of E reviews wedding ban on divorcees
>
> Cabinet will end 'quickie' divorces
>
> Divorced wives may get half of pension money
>
> divorcees
>
> House blown up in divorce battle
>
> ivorce
>
> Mackay seeks end to 'quickie' divorces
>
> Three runaway sisters try to mend their parents' broken marriage

A What do you think causes most marriages to break up?

c) Divorce is immoral because it introduces disorder into the family and society. Divorce harms the following people:

  ❖ The spouse who has been deserted by his or her partner. The CCC points out that there is a considerable difference between a partner who has sincerely tried to remain faithful, only to find themselves deserted, and one who has broken the marriage vows.

  ❖ Children, who suffer greatly from the separation of their parents and the emotional conflict involved in choosing between them.

  ❖ Society, because divorce spreads like a plague and convinces many people that they too can break their marriage vows.

B *This is an African one parent family. The majority of one parent families are brought about by divorce. What special problems do one parent families face all over the world?*

Annulment and separation

The Catholic Church does not grant divorces. In exceptional circumstances, however, it does grant an annulment. The effect of an annulment is to declare that the marriage never officially existed. There are 12 grounds on which an annulment might be granted. These include:

❖ One of the partners not consenting to the marriage in the first place.

❖ One spouse not understanding the implications of what they were doing when they married.

❖ The marriage not being consummated – sexual intercourse not having taken place.

Separation may be a painful, but necessary, answer to a marriage that has become unworkable. This can lead to a civil divorce without any blame being attached to either partner. In this way certain legal rights, the care of the children and any inheritance can be protected.

FIND OUT AND NOTE ...

Jesus had more to say about divorce than almost any other social issue. Look up the following references, make notes on them in your books and then answer the questions.

a) **Matthew 5.31-32**
  ❖ Why do you think that a man who divorces his wife turns her into an adulteress?
  ❖ What appears to be the one exception to this rule?

b) **Matthew 19.3-9**
  ❖ On what basis does Jesus dismiss the possibility of divorce in these verses?

c) **Mark 10.9**
  ❖ Can you find out whether a woman was allowed to divorce her husband in the time of Jesus?

d) **1.Corinthians 7.10,11**
  ❖ How does Paul try to invest his words about divorce and adultery with extra authority?

ANSWER IN YOUR BOOK ...

1 Why is adultery condemned by the Roman Catholic Church without reservation?

2 Why is divorce unacceptable to the Roman Catholic Church?

3 What harm does divorce do?

IN THE GLOSSARY ...

Old Testament; Adultery; New Testament; Prophet; Catholic Church.

7.5. SEX (1)

The Catholic Church believes that sexual intercourse should be confined to marriage. Sex outside marriage is a serious mis-use of one of God's greatest gifts, trivialising and spoiling an activity which can be the source of great blessing. Instead of confirming and supporting a couple's love for each other, sex outside marriage only encourages selfishness.

Given that God has created us, issues relating to our sexuality are bound to play an important part in our lives. We are, after all, a unity of body and soul, with every part of that unity being affected by our sexuality. God's intention is that the differences between the two sexes are expressed in marriage and family life. The success of a marriage, and the happiness of the two people within it, depend to a large extent on their ability to come to terms with these differences. Within a marriage these include the following:

a) Our feelings for one another.
b) Our capacity to love each other.
c) Our desire to procreate (have children).

Chastity

Chastity (abstaining from sex) is the normal attitude which Catholics should adopt towards sexual activity. It takes various forms in different situations:

1. For married people it refers to the limitation of sexual activity to one's partner. The CCC calls this 'conjugal chastity'. As we learnt in Unit 7.3, such faithfulness should be normal for all Christian marriages.
2. For widows, chastity is abstaining from sex unless they re-marry.
3. For virgins, chastity means that they should not engage in sexual activity until they are married. This includes those who are engaged to be married. They should look on their engagement period as a time of testing in which they discover:

> "... a mutual respect, an apprenticeship in fidelity and the hope of receiving one another from God." (CCC 2350)

A *Do you think that it is realistic to expect this young couple to be chaste until after they marry?*

Chastity does not come naturally to human beings. It is a gift of God that only comes when a person learns to master their own body through self-discipline. Sexual feelings are so strong that if we do not control them, they will control us. By bringing our sexual feelings under control, we are being faithful to our baptismal vows. While such self-control is difficult at any time, it is particularly difficult when our sexual feelings are at their strongest – during adolescence and early adulthood.

Why live a chaste life? This is a particularly important question in an age when comparatively few people appear to want to control their sexual feelings. The Catholic Church teaches that the benefits of chastity are considerable:

a) They enable a Christian to follow in the footsteps of Jesus. Jesus was a model of chastity for all Christians to follow. As St Paul wrote:

"All baptised in Christ, you have all clothed yourselves in Christ…" (Galatians 3.27)

B *What is the link between living a chaste life and spiritual growth in the Catholic faith?*

b) Chastity is part of a person's growth towards holiness. The stages along this pathway are often marked by imperfection and frequently by sin. Yet, day by day, a person can find their Christian life strengthened if they make the right choices. As we learn to know and appreciate chastity better, we will want to tread its paths more often.

ANSWER IN YOUR BOOK …

1 What do you think Roman Catholics mean when they speak of the 'soul'?

2 What is 'chastity' and what different forms does it take?

3 What are the benefits of living a chaste life?

IN YOUR OWN WORDS …

St Ambrose was a Bishop in the early Christian Church. He wrote this statement:

"There are three forms of the virtue of chastity: the first is that of spouses, the second that of widows and the third that of virgins. We do not praise any of them to the exclusion of the others… This is what makes for the richness of the discipline of the Church…"

a) What does chastity mean for the following:
❖ Those who are married?
❖ Those who are widowed?
❖ Those who are virgins?

b) What do you think St Ambrose meant when he said: "This is what makes for the richness of the discipline of the Church…"?

DISCUSS AMONG YOURSELVES …

a) Why do you think that the Catholic Church strongly maintains that sexual intercourse should be confined to marriage?

b) Why do you think that sexual activity should only be practised by married people with their partners?

c) Why do you think that everyone should firmly control their sexual appetite?

IN THE GLOSSARY …

Chastity; Catholic Church; St Paul.

7.6 SEX (2)

All baptised Christians have a vocation from God. Whatever their situation, they are expected to live a life of 'chastity'. In order to do this, they must be acutely aware of those practices and activities which are contrary to a chaste life. The CCC lists them as follows:

a) *Lust*. Lust is the desire for sexual pleasure without any commitment being involved. Pure lust encourages someone to treat another person only as a sexual object. As Jesus made clear (Matthew 5.27,28), lust begins in the mind. It is a form of mental adultery.

b) *Masturbation*. This is the deliberate stimulation of the sexual organs simply to give oneself sexual pleasure. The Church has always maintained that masturbation is an 'intrinsically and gravely disordered action.' The deliberate mis-use of the sexual organs outside of marriage is an act of impurity. This is not to say that all acts of masturbation are seen by the Church as being equally sinful. The young and immature, together with those who are under a considerable personal strain, should not be judged too harshly for masturbating. Having said that, masturbation is always wrong because it is not a union of one flesh, but a solitary act outside of any male-female relationship.

c) *Fornication*. This is a sexual relationship between an unmarried man and woman. In the New Testament, it is listed alongside such immoral actions as murder, theft and adultery. The Roman Catholic Church considers it to be wrong because the idea of 'the two becoming one body' is not possible outside the commitment of marriage.

d) *Pornography*. Sexual activity should be carried out in private. Pornography is putting private sexual actions and behaviour on public display. To do so degrades everyone involved, irrespective of whether they are actors, models, photographers or the public who look at it. Pornography turns sex into a nasty, commercial activity, far removed from the love and care which should be its main characteristics.

e) *Prostitution*. This does a grave injury to the man or woman involved and to the person who pays for sexual services. Both defile the body, which is the temple of the Holy Spirit. Although it is shameful to be a prostitute the blame is lessened if poverty or blackmail are involved.

f) *Rape*. This is a very serious crime indeed. The rapist forces sexual activity on another person, normally a woman. By so doing, it goes a long way towards destroying a person's self-respect. The victim can be marked for life. The rape of children by parents (incest) or by other adults is the worst sexual crime of all. Indeed, any sexual activity which involves the use of children is to be totally and unreservedly condemned.

A *How would you describe society's present attitude towards sex, as indicated in these newspaper headlines?*

Teenage thoughts on food, drugs and sex
Plea for more aid for young sex offenders
Cardinal silent on sex claims
Children's claims of sexual abuse 'drew on videos'
Cadet leader had sex with girl, 14
Sex claims totally untrue, dean tells congregation
Boy blames father's death mother's affair
I'm not an adulterer, Dean tells cathedral
Families cleared of sex abuse go home to their shattered lives
Runaway 'slaves' tell of sex abuse and attacks
" **Elvis had a voice that could explain the sexuality of America.**"
Legalise sex for sale, say nurses
Pope condemns 'rampant porn'
TV porn channel wins UK licence
Inquiry into sex abuse at boys' homes
ne woman pilot ndured endless sexual taunts'
Doctor made 'honest error' on abortions
Tribunal backs decision to sack sex-pest lecturer
Sex-case Pc cleared
Power and money turn men into adulterers
lice 'smash multi-million pornography ring'
for sex

Homosexuality

A homosexual is someone, male or female, who feels sexually attracted to members of their own, rather than the opposite, sex. Even today, scientists are far from sure why 1 in every 15 people in the population are homosexual.

The Bible takes a strong line against homosexuality (see Genesis 19.1-29; Romans 1.24-27; 1.Corinthians 6.10; 1.Timothy 1.10) and Church tradition has supported this opposition. It has maintained for centuries that homosexual acts are 'intrinsically disordered'. By acting unnaturally, homosexuals close the sexual act to the possibility of creating life. The CCC concludes:

"Under no circumstances can they be approved." (2359)

So what about homosexual people? How should they be treated? They should be treated with respect, compassion and sensitivity. As Christians, they should bring their condition to God and find the spiritual strength to cope with it. This will allow them to live a chaste life. Through prayer and the sacraments they can overcome any problems that their condition brings upon them.

> **B** *Try to find out more about the attitude of the Roman Catholic Church to homosexuality.*

ANSWER IN YOUR BOOK ...

1 Which two sexual activities are expressly described as being 'intrinsically and gravely disordered'? Can you explain why?

2 Why have pornography and prostitution been described as 'naked exploitation'?

3 Why has the Church always been opposed to homosexuality?

WHAT DO YOU THINK?

Look again at the list of sexual activities to which the Church is totally opposed. Think about them. Does it not seem strange to you that a comparatively harmless activity like masturbation can be linked with such serious sexual crimes as rape? Do you consider all the activities to be 'harmful'? Perhaps you would like to divide them up into a) Serious activities ...and b) Less serious activities? Which would you place in each group?

WRITE AN ESSAY ...

Write about 400 words on the title 'The Bible, the Church and homosexuality'.

IN THE GLOSSARY ...

Chastity; New Testament; Homosexuality; Roman Catholic Church; Holy Spirit; Bible; Sacrament.

7.7 RESPECT FOR HUMAN LIFE

Several passages in the Old and New Testaments underline the distinctive Jewish, and Christian, understanding of human life. One such passage is Genesis 1.26-27 (Refer to READ AND DECIDE...) and if you read it carefully you will notice two important points:

1 *Men and women are made in the 'image of God'.* All other forms of life were created before human beings. After each form of life was brought into being we are told that God 'saw that it was good'. Nothing, however, was actually created in the 'image of God'.

   Men and women are said to be different – even unique. They are both said to bear a striking likeness to God, although we are obviously not talking about a physical likeness here as God is pure Spirit. The reference is to the spiritual relationship which human beings share with God and which no other form of life can enjoy. It is this which makes it possible for there to be a unique communion between the Divine and the human.

2 *Man has a 'dominion' over all other forms of life.* This uniqueness gives men and women an authority which extends over all nature. It stems from humankind's superior intelligence and genuine freedom. Humankind can shape events whilst the rest of nature can only respond to them. Power, however, always brings responsibility and man must exercise his authority responsibly. He must treat nature just as God treats man.

Why respect human life?

Man, then, must respect all forms of life. In particular, he must show the greatest possible respect for human life. There are several reasons for this:

❖ All men and women are made in God's image.
❖ All human beings are created equal by God. No one group cannot treat another as inferior.
❖ When Jesus died on the cross it was for the salvation of every human being – without exception.
❖ Every human being has an 'immortal' soul, the welfare of which is in the hands of God alone. No-one has the right to end another human being's life prematurely.
❖ Just as God alone decides when conception takes place, so he alone can determine the moment of a person's death.

A A hunt in progress. Do you think that this way of behaving is in keeping with man's responsibility to the whole of creation?

> **B** *In which areas of life do you think the Church should act to protect the poor, disadvantaged and homeless? Find out about the activities of the Roman Catholic Church in one of these areas.*

The implications of these beliefs are considerable. They affect the way in which Catholics approach a whole range of social issues. These will be discussed in detail in the chapters that follow but two preliminary observations can be made here:

a) Whatever a human being's age, state of health, educational achievements, intelligence-level or place in society is, they can, and do, make a unique contribution to the well-being of society. Their value is God-given.

b) The Church must be totally opposed to all forms of discrimination as this depends on judging some individuals to be less valuable than others. This means, for instance, that the physically and mentally handicapped must be looked after by society, even though they can never make any economic contribution to that society. The Church must constantly be on its guard to protect those who cannot protect themselves. As a consequence, the Catholic Church is totally opposed to all unnatural forms of birth-control (Unit 7.8); abortion (Unit 7.9); euthanasia (Unit 7.10) and suicide (Unit 7.11).

ANSWER IN YOUR BOOK ...

1 In which ways do Catholics believe that human beings are different from all other forms of life?

2 What authority does the human race have? How should that authority be properly exercised?

3 Why do Catholics believe that all forms of human life are to be respected and safeguarded?

WHAT DO YOU THINK?

a) What does it mean in practice to speak of men and women being made in the image of God?

b) What does it mean when we speak of all human beings as being infinitely precious?

c) Why do you think that the Church must be opposed to all forms of discrimination against other human beings?

READ AND DECIDE ...

In Genesis 1.26-27 we read these words:
"God said, 'Let us make man in our own image, in the likeness of ourselves, and let them be masters of the fish of the sea, the birds of the heaven, the cattle, all the wild beasts and all the reptiles that crawl upon the earth',
God created man in the image of himself,
in the image of God he created him,
male and female he created them."

a) What does the text mean when it says 'God created man in the image of himself'?

b) How do you understand the directive '... let them be masters of the ...' What kind of dominion are we talking about here? What do you think are the limitations placed upon the power of the human race?

IN THE GLOSSARY ...

Old Testament; New Testament; Soul; Catholic Church; Birth-control; Abortion; Euthanasia.

7.8 BIRTH-CONTROL

The love between a husband and a wife lends itself naturally towards having children since a baby comes from the very heart of that relationship. New life both fulfils and completes that love. The Catholic Church, which is always on the side of life, teaches that, in the words of Pope Paul VI:

> "… each and every marriage act must remain open to the transmission of life…"

Married couples should see this as one of the the most important parts of their relationship. Their true vocation together is to create new life. When they do so they are co-operating with the love of God, their Creator, and sharing in the fatherhood of God – as Ephesians 3.14 and Matthew 23.9 indicate.

A *These nuns are discussing birth control at a conference. Can you find out why the christian churches were traditionally opposed to birth control?*

The regulation of birth

Until the 1930s, all of the major Christian Churches were opposed to birth-control or 'birth regulation' as it was then called. The first Lambeth Conference of the Anglican Church after the First World War (1914-18), for instance, taught that the use of contraception was morally and spiritually wrong. During his short reign (1958-63) Pope John XXIII set up a commission to look into the whole question of birth-control and family planning. After Pope Paul VI had succeeded Pope John XXIII the commission presented two reports – one from a majority of its members and the other from a minority.

The majority report recommended a change in the Catholic Church's traditional opposition to all means of contraception. The minority urged the Pope to hold fast to the traditional teaching. Pope Paul VI supported the minority view and, in 1968, published the Papal encyclical 'Humanae Vitae' (On the Regulation of Birth). All forms of artificial birth-control, such as the pill and the condom, were outlawed together with sterilisation. Only 'natural' forms of contraception were permitted. The encyclical was, to say the least, controversial. In some countries, such as Great Britain and the USA, surveys suggest that as many as 80% of Roman Catholics do not support the teaching of the Church on this matter.

The arguments for the Catholic Church's ban on artificial means of contraception can be briefly outlined as follows:

a) The Church has always taught that it is wrong to interfere with the natural processes of conception and birth. If the Church has been wrong on this particular issue for so long, the authority of the 'magisterium' would be called into question.

b) 'Natural laws' exist which govern all moral behaviour. These 'laws' have been put in place by God to govern all human behaviour. If an activity is against the natural law then it must be wrong. As God has intended every act of sexual intercourse to be open to the possibility of creating new life, it is immoral to interfere with that.

c) Contraception is wrong because of the effect it has upon sexual intercourse. It turns an act which is intended to create new life into one which is purely for the pleasure of the two people involved.

Natural family planning

So far we have only been referring to 'unnatural' or 'artificial' means of contraception. The Church does, however, consider it to be permissable to take advantage of those times in a

B *Can you find out more about Natural Family Planning?*

month when a woman is not fertile to limit the number of babies she conceives. This is a method of birth-control (Natural Family Planning) which does not make use of any external devices, has no side-effects and costs nothing.

ANSWER IN YOUR BOOK ...

1 What, according to the Catholic Church, is the most important purpose of marriage?

2 What was Humanae Vitae and why was it important in the Catholic Church?

3 What are the main arguments in favour of the Church's ban on artificial methods of birth-control?

WHAT DO YOU THINK?

a) What does the Church mean when it says that it is always on the side of life? In which areas, apart from contraception, could this principle be applied?

b) What does the Church mean when it says that sexual intercourse should always be open to the possibility of new life?

c) What does the Church mean when it refers to artificial means of birth-control as 'unnatural'?

d) What does the Church mean when it claims that to change its mind over birth-control would undermine the teaching authority of the magisterium?

FIND OUT AND NOTE ...

Contraception has been a very important topic of debate in the Catholic Church for over 25 years and remains so today. Try to invite two Roman Catholics, with opposing viewpoints on the issue, to outline the main arguments for you? After listening to what they have to say, try to decide whether you think the Church might change its mind over birth-control in the near future.

IN THE GLOSSARY ...

Pope; Magisterium; Vocation; Catholic Church; Birth-control; Anglican Church; Contraception; Pope John XXIII; Pill; Condom; Sterilisation.

7.9 ABORTION

Abortion is an operation carried out to remove the growing foetus from its mother's womb so that it can be destroyed. In the U.K, abortion has been legal since 1967, providing certain conditions are met. An abortion can legally be carried out if the following occurs:

1 It is performed before the 24th week of pregnancy – the 28th week until 1991.
2 Two doctors agree that it is undesirable for the pregnancy to continue on personal, social or medical grounds.
3 It is thought likely that the continuation of the pregnancy would endanger the physical, or psychological, health of the mother or her family.

A *This group of people are in favour of abortion. What do you think the Roman Catholic Church would say against their cause?*

Since 1967 around 140,000 abortions have been carried out each year in the U.K. and this number shows no signs of diminishing. 10% of people who obtain an abortion here have travelled from other countries where the operation is illegal.

Abortion and the Roman Catholic Church

Two organisations, SPUC (The Society for the Protection of the Unborn Child) and LIFE, have campaigned strongly against abortion since 1967. In this they have had the wholehearted support of the Roman Catholic Church, whose leaders have made the Church's fundamental objection to abortion very clear. They have pointed out the following:

a) Abortion denies the most fundamental right of all – the right to exist. The matter is made much worse, of course, by the fact that this right is being denied to the most vulnerable group of all in our society: babies that are still in their mother's wombs.

b) Life begins the moment that a baby is conceived in the womb. This means that there is no real difference between abortion and murder.

The Church has always been opposed to abortion. The Didache, the earliest Christian document still surviving, had this to say:

> "You shall not kill the embryo and shall not cause the newborn to perish."

'Infanticide'(killing babies just born) was a fairly common practice when the Church was born. This used to take place if the child did not suit the family's requirements. Various Church documents over the centuries have linked abortion and infanticide, and roundly condemned them both. As 'Gaudium et Spes', one such document, declares:

> "Life must be protected with the utmost care from the moment of conception; Abortion and infanticide are abominable crimes."

Indeed, so serious has the crime of abortion been considered to be that the Church has, in the past, threatened anyone involved in an abortion with excommunication. This is the heaviest penalty that the Church can impose on people since it bars them from receiving the Sacraments. Even bearing this in mind, the crime is far greater than the punishment when one considers the following:

- ❖ the irreparable harm done to the innocent baby who is put to death;
- ❖ the harm done to the baby's parents who have taken part in an act of murder;
- ❖ the harm done to a society which places such a low value on human life.

In recent years the Roman Catholic Church has formed a strong alliance with the Evangelical wing in the Protestant Churches to oppose abortion under any circumstances – a position called 'Pro-Life'. Although approaching the matter from very different Christian viewpoints, both of these groups bring an over-riding respect for human life to the discussion. This respect extends not only to the unborn baby but also to the handicapped, the elderly and any other group which needs protection in a civilised society.

ANSWER IN YOUR BOOK ...

1 What is the law relating to abortion in the U.K?

2 Can you find out why Roman Catholics maintain that life begins at the moment of conception?

3 Why is the Roman Catholic Church so strongly opposed to abortion?

DISCUSS AMONG YOURSELVES ...

The whole debate about abortion is very heated. Here are some things for you to think about and discuss with one another:

a) When does the foetus become a human being? While those opposed to abortion believe that it is at the moment of conception, others argue that it is not until the foetus is fully formed. Consult Jeremiah 1.5; Job 10.8-12 and Psalm 22.10-11 before making up your mind.

b) People who support abortion claim that a woman has the ultimate right over what happens to her body. The Roman Catholic counter-claim is that the unborn baby has rights which are at least equal to those of its mother. What do you think?

c) Ultimately, the Roman Catholic position on abortion depends on the belief that every baby conceived is a gift from God. Can you think of any situations in which it is very difficult to maintain this? What answer do you think the Roman Catholic Church might give?

B Can you explain why people against abortion call themselves 'Pro-Life'?

IN THE GLOSSARY ...

Bible; Excommunication; Sacrament; Protestant; Abortion.

7.10 EUTHANASIA

Euthanasia (mercy-killing) is illegal in Great Britain. In fact, the only country in Europe where euthanasia is legal is Holland, which allows it under certain strict conditions. Euthanasia extends to a person the right to have their life ended if they have a terminal illness or a condition which prevents them from living a meaningful life. The actual decision to end the life can take two forms:

1 A decision taken by the person concerned when they have all their faculties, laying down the conditions under which they would want their life terminated in the future.
2 A decision at the time taken on the patient's behalf by doctors and their relatives.

Few people would deny that life and death decisions are being taken by doctors every day. Sometimes these decisions may verge on the edge of euthanasia although they mainly involve the withholding of medical treatment rather than taking active steps to end a person's life.

It is important to point out that there is a marked difference between 'compulsory' euthanasia and 'voluntary' euthanasia. Compulsory euthanasia has been used as the tool of fascist governments, as we saw with the Nazis in the Second World War. No-one for a moment is suggesting that the life of anyone should be ended compulsorily. Those who support euthanasia are arguing that it should be available for those who want it.

Euthanasia – the Church and the issues

The Church's concern is to bring the light and life of Christ to everyone who needs it. It teaches clearly that those whose lives are diminished or weakened in any way should be treated with special care. In particular, the sick, the handicapped and the elderly should be helped to live as normal a life as possible. Whatever its motives, euthanasia does mean putting a premature end to the lives of such people. In any civilised society it is morally unacceptable to even contemplate the possibility. Why is it unacceptable? Here are four reasons:

a) Euthanasia is murder.
b) Euthanasia is contrary to the dignity of human beings.
c) Euthanasia destroys the respect that is due to God, the Beginning and End of all life.
d) There is a clear difference between discontinuing treatment and actively killing someone. There are certain situations in which one simply cannot prevent the eventuality of death. These must be recognised and the decision to end treatment taken in consultation with the patient, if at all possible. If not, then the closest relative(s) should be involved.

A   A new hospice is being built. The demand for places, however, is far greater than the availability of beds. Why do you think so many people want hospice care at the end of their days?

Obviously, the care of people who are terminally ill is very demanding. Painkillers should be used wisely to bring relief to the patient. Their use is justified, even if by using them a doctor shortens the life of the patient. Every step should be taken to help the patient face death with true dignity.

Hospices

Hospices have been at the forefront of providing care for those people who are terminally ill in the 20th century. Many of them have been staffed by Roman Catholics, nuns and lay-people. Hospice treatment is based upon the belief that pain can always be controlled, even when a disease has reached a very advanced state. With the pain under control the person can then learn how to face up to their own impending death with true dignity. More widespread hospice care, not euthanasia, is the answer for those coming to the end of their natural life.

ANSWER IN YOUR BOOK ...

1 What is euthanasia?
2 What is the difference between 'compulsory' and 'voluntary' euthanasia?
3 What is distinctive about the hospice movement?

WHAT DO YOU THINK?

Euthanasia is a very emotive issue. Here are some questions for you to think about and discuss:

a) Most people see a clear distinction between a doctor withholding treatment from a patient who is dying, and actively administering a drug to hasten their death. Do you see the difference? If wo, can you try to explain what it is?

b) Would describing euthanasia as murder be an exaggeration? How would you describe it?

c) If a person has been certified as 'brain dead' after an accident and their life-support machine turned off, is that euthanasia? Is it murder?

FIND OUT AND NOTE ...

Is there a hospice near to you? If so, can you arrange for someone from the hospice to visit your class? There is a great deal of interesting and important information that you need to find out. In particular, try to discover how the hospice helps people come to terms with the final stages of their life.

IN THE GLOSSARY ...

Euthanasia; Hospice; Nun.

7.11 SUICIDE

Both the Holy Scriptures and the Tradition of the Church tell us that all human life is sacred (holy). Abortion and euthanasia are wrong because we have been told by Christ to love both our neighbours and ourselves (Matthew 19.19). Taking its lead from this teaching of Jesus, the Catholic Church has always maintained that we are not masters of our own fate. Our lives are in the hands of God. God alone chose the moment that we entered this world and He will choose the moment that we leave it. Our responsibility is to administer lives which we have been given by God as stewards. This means that we must accept our lives thankfully as a gift and preserve it for the honour of God and the salvation of our souls. It follows, then, that we cannot simply dispose of our lives when we want to. If we commit suicide we take on board a decision which God alone should make.

Suicide

The CCC makes several important points about suicide:

a) Everyone must take responsibility for their own life because, at the Last Judgment, we will be answerable to God for it.
b) Suicide is not only wrong. It is also unnatural. The natural inclination for every form of life, human and non-human, is to preserve life at all costs. Suicide is an intensely selfish act. Not only do we destroy ourselves but we also cause great pain and heartache to our relatives and friends. Suicide is contrary to the life of love which God has called upon all believers to follow.
c) In the world in which we live for a short period of time, God has called upon us to be examples for others to follow. What kind of example does suicide set? Who can comprehend the impact that the act has upon those who love us, especially our children? What are they likely to think and feel as they grow up?

To take one's own life is a grave sin. It is an equally serious sin for a person to help someone to take their own life. If euthanasia was ever legalised, this would also include the doctors and nurses involved.

However, as the CCC points out, not every act of suicide carries equal blame. Who can even begin to understand what is going through the mind of a

A *Many people come to the Clifton Suspension Bridge to end their lives. What do you think might bring these people to the position where life no longer seems to be worth living?*

B Try to find out about the Samaritans organisation. When was it founded? What does it do? How many people does it help each year?

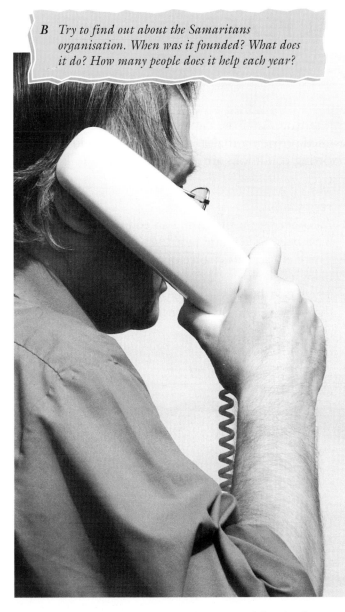

person who is driven to take their own life? As the CCC states:

> "Grave psychological disturbances, anguish or grave fear of hardship, suffering or torture can diminish the responsibility of the one committing suicide." (2282)

Surely God will take into account the pressures which lead someone to take their own life? This should be an enormous comfort to the friends and relatives who remain. They should not worry about the eternal salvation of those who have committed suicide. This is a matter which can be safely left in God's hands. He can be trusted to provide such people in the after-life with the opportunity to repent for what they have done.

Meanwhile, those left behind on earth should not judge those who have committed suicide too harshly. All that the Catholic Church can do is to commit such people to 'Our Lady of Sorrows' – the Virgin Mary.

ANSWER IN YOUR BOOK ...

1 What is a human being's responsibility to God for his or her own life?

2 Why does the Roman Catholic Church treat suicide as a sin?

3 What reassurance does the Church offer to those left behind after a suicide?

WHAT DO YOU THINK?

For a very long time the Catholic Church treated suicide as a scandal. Many churches refused to conduct a burial service for those who had committed suicide. They would not even bury them in consecrated ground. Why do you think that the Church took such a strong stand over suicide? What do you think has happened to make them relax their attitude?

USE YOUR IMAGINATION ...

Suicide has an enormous impact upon those who loved the deceased. Put yourselves in the position of the following:

a) A husband or wife whose partner has committed suicide.

b) The son or daughter of a father or mother who has committed suicide.

After their death, what questions do you think you would need to have answered? How do you think you might begin to come to terms with the situation? What do you think your feelings might be towards the person who had taken their own life? Would you blame them?

IN THE GLOSSARY ...

Holy Scriptures; Abortion; Euthanasia; Last Judgement; Catholic Church; Soul; Virgin Mary.

7.12 WAR AND PEACE

All Christian Churches have been responsible for war and violence in the past and the Catholic Church is no exception. Its position today is that while war is always regrettable it can, under certain conditions, be morally and spiritually justified. We will look at these conditions shortly.

The Just War

No-one should be able to find glory in war, especially modern warfare. The amount of destruction that we can now inflict on others makes it very difficult to justify any war. Since the time of St Thomas Aquinas in the 13th century, however, there has always been a Just War tradition in the Roman Catholic Church. Taking its lead from Aquinas, the Church teaches that a war is justified providing that it is in self defence and that the following conditions are met:

1 The damage inflicted by an enemy is lasting and very serious.
2 All other means of putting an end to the aggression have been tried – and failed.
3 There is a serious chance of a war against the enemy being effective.
4 The bloodshed brought about by the war is less than that caused by the previous aggression.

A *What do you think could possibly justify scenes like this?*

152

Only the legitimate government of a country can declare war. Even so, it must work out the full implications of this decision before it embarks on any counter attack.

Fighting a war

A war will be fought by those in the armed forces. These forces exist to maintain the common good of the people and the peace of their country. If their country goes to war, those in the armed forces are not free to use any means that they choose in combat. Their weapons must always be directed against other soldiers, not civilian targets. This is a very important principle since the nature of warfare has changed dramatically in the 20th century. During the First World War (1914-18), for instance, less than 10% of those killed were civilians. In more than 250 armed conflicts which have been waged since the Second World War ended in 1945, more than 90% of those killed have been civilians.

Pacifism

When a country goes to war there will always be those who object to it both on moral and religious grounds. They are called 'conscientious objectors'. By not fighting they are committing themselves to 'pacifism', an attitude which does not condone the use of violence in any situation. Unlike the Protestant Church, the Roman Catholic Church does not have a strong pacifist tradition. The CCC states that those who cannot find it within themselves to serve their country by fighting must find some community work to do instead.

Having laid down the conditions under which a war should be fought, the Roman Catholic Church places itself firmly on the side of those striving for peace. All citizens and governments, the CCC declares, are obliged to work for the avoidance of war. The Second Vatican Council declared that the Church should be working for the following:

a) *The abolition of the Arms Race.* The world's super-powers spend enormous sums of money developing bigger and better weapons – and then try to sell them to other countries. This is referred to as the Arms Race and, according to the Second Vatican Council, is immoral.

b) *The abolition of nuclear weapons.* Everything that has been said about a just war would be irrelevant if nuclear weapons were ever used. Such weapons not only threaten individual nations but the future of the whole world. Catholics should work tirelessly for a better future by committing themselves to working towards the abolition of nuclear weapons everywhere.

ANSWER IN YOUR BOOK ...

1 What is a 'Just War'? What are the principles under which such a war can be fought?

2 What is 'pacifism'? Who are the 'conscientious objectors'?

3 What did the Second Vatican Council call for to improve the security of the world?

READ AND DECIDE ...

Here are two quotations from the CCC. Read them carefully and answer the questions:

a) "The mere fact that war has regrettably broken out does not mean that everything becomes elicit (lawful) between the warring parties." (2312)
   ❖ What activities do you think are totally unacceptable in a war situation? Why?

b) "The arms race is one of the greatest curses on the human race and the harm it inflicts on the poor is more than can be endured." (2329)
   ❖ What is the 'arms race'? Why does it inflict so much damage on the world's poor?

WHAT DO YOU THINK?

Here are two quotations from the Bible:

❖ "... they shall beat their swords into ploughshares and their spears into pruning hooks; nation shall not lift up sword against nation, neither shall they learn war any more." (Isaiah 2.4)

❖ Blessed are the peacemakers, for they shall be called sons of God." (Matthew 5.27-28)

a) What do you think 'peace' is?

b) What point do you think the quotation from Isaiah 2.4 is making?

c) Why do you think that the reward for peacemakers in the quotation from Matthew 5.27-28 is so high?

IN THE GLOSSARY ...

Catholic Church; Just War; Second Vatican Council.

THE GLOSSARY

A

Abbot – the title of the Superior (leader) of a Benedictine monastery or abbey.

Abortion – the removal and destruction before the end of a pregnancy of the growing foetus (baby) from its mother's womb.

Absolution – the declaration by a priest that a person's sins are forgiven by God.

Acts of the Apostles – the book in the New Testament which records the early history of the Christian Church.

Adultery – sexual relations by a married person with someone other than their marriage partner.

Advent – (coming) – the period of preparation leading up to the festival of Christmas.

Altar – the stone or wooden platform behind which the priest stands during the Eucharist or the Mass.

Anglican Church – the worldwide Church of England.

Anointing the sick – anointing those who are sick, or near to death, with oil which has been blessed by the bishop.

Anti-semitism – any form of hatred directed solely against the Jews.

Apocrypha – the books accepted by the Catholic Church as 'deuterocanonical' and included in the Bible between the Old and New Testaments.

Apostle – someone who 'is sent', referring specifically to the twelve disciples of Jesus after the resurrection.

Apostles Creed – the statement of belief used in the Catholic Church from about 390 CE onwards.

Apostolic Succession – the Catholic belief that the authority given to the original disciples has been passed down through successive Popes.

Ascension Day – the day which celebrates the ascension of Jesus into heaven.

Ash Wednesday – the first day of Lent.

Assumption of the Blessed Virgin – the belief held by Catholics that, at her death, the Virgin Mary was taken directly, body and soul, into heaven.

B

Baptism – the Catholic rite of initiation into the faith carried out on babies or adults.

Beatific Vision – the eternal vision of God granted to those who have reached heaven.

Benedictines – the Religious Order founded by St Benedict about 530 CE.

Bible – the collection of sacred writings which form the basis of the Catholic faith.

Birth-control – the controlling of the number of babies born by artificial means.

Bishop – the highest of the three Orders in the Catholic priesthood – the other two being deacon and priest.

Bishop of Rome – the position in the Catholic Church first held by St Peter and then by successive Popes.

C

Canon of Scripture – the list of books in the Bible recognised as authoritative by the Church.

Cardinal – the most important bishops in the Catholic Church.

Catechism – an elementary introduction to the Catholic faith which is often written in a question and answer form.

Catholic Church – the Catholic (universal) Church is that Church which traces its origins back to the original Apostles.

Celibacy – the acceptance of a permanent unmarried state as a vocation from God.

Chastity – the rejection of all sexual relations outside marriage.

Chrism – the consecrated oil used by the Catholic Church for its Sacraments.

Chrismation – the service in the Orthodox Church which brings together baptism and confirmation.

Christmas – the festival which celebrates the birth of Jesus.

Church – the term which is used to describe the community of Christians throughout the world, one particular branch of the worldwide Church or a building in which Christians meet.

Church Council – a meeting of church bishops and other leaders who are called together by the Pope.

Cistercians – the Order of White Monks, formed in 1098 by Robert de Molesme.

Clergy – those called to be ordained.

Communion of Saints – the fellowship of each Christian with Christ and, through him, with saints in heaven and on earth.

Condom – a plastic covering placed over the penis during sexual intercourse to prevent conception.

Confession – the acknowledgement of one's sins to God, usually carried out through a priest.

Confessional box – the traditional place where confession takes place.

Confirmation – the service which admits a person into full membership of the Catholic Church.

Contemplation – a form of mental prayer.

Contraception – any artificial means of effectively preventing conception.

Convent – the building in which a community of nuns live.

Council of Trent – the Church Council, held in the 16th Century, which laid down teachings accepted by the Church until the First Vatican Council.

Creed – an official statement of Christian belief.

Crucifix – a model of a cross which carries an image of the crucified Christ.

D

Day of Obligation – Holy Days throughout the year when Catholics are obliged to attend church.

Day of Pentecost – the day on which the Holy Spirit was given to the early Christian believers and the Church was born.

Deacon – the first of three Orders in the Church – the others being priest and bishop.

Denomination – any Christian Church.

Devil – the supreme power of evil, also called Satan.

Diocese – the area over which a single bishop has authority.

Disciple – a follower who accepts the 'discipline' of their teacher.

Divine Liturgy – the Greek Orthodox order of service for the Eucharist.

E

Easter – the festival at which Christians celebrate the death and resurrection of Jesus.

Easter Sunday – the day on which Christians celebrate the rising of Jesus from the dead.

Epiphany – the Christian festival, held on January 6th, to celebrate the 'manifestation' (showing) of Jesus to the Wise Men.

Episcopacy – a system of Church government headed by bishops.

Epistles – letters which are included in the New Testament.

Eucharist – the service of 'thanksgiving' which celebrates the death of Jesus. Also known as 'Holy Communion' or the 'Mass'.

Euthanasia – (mercy-killing) – the right of people to have their lives ended prematurely.

Ex Cathedra – (from the throne) – when the Pope speaks as the successor of St Peter his words become the official teaching of the Church.

Excommunication – the power of the Catholic Church to exclude heretics from participation in the sacraments.

Exodus – the journey of the Israelites out of Egyptian slavery in the Old Testament.

F

Fall – the eating by the first man and woman of the forbidden fruit in the Garden of Eden.

Fasting – going without food for religious reasons.

First Vatican Council – the Council of the Catholic Church held between 1869 and 1871.

Font – the stone receptacle which holds the water for infant baptism.

Franciscans – the Religious Order founded by St Francis of Assissi.

G

Gentile – a non-Jew.

Good Friday – the day on which Christians remember the crucifixion of Jesus.

Gospel – the 'Good News' of the salvation brought by Jesus.

Gospels – the books in the New Testament which contain a record of the life, teaching and death of Jesus.

Great Schism – the event, in 1054, which led to the breaking of all relations between the Catholic and Orthodox Churches.

H

Hail Mary – a very important Catholic prayer to the Virgin Mary.

Heaven – the term used to describe the home of God and the angels – and the eventual destination of all believers.

Hell – the term used to describe the home of Satan and all his followers.

Heretic – someone who teaches beliefs which are contrary to the teachings of the Catholic Church.

Hermit – a person who lives a life of prayer on their own.

Holy Communion – the popular Anglican term to describe the Eucharist or the Mass.

Holy Saturday – the day between Good Friday and Easter Sunday.

Holy Scriptures – the sacred writings which make up the Bible.

Holy Spirit – the third person in the Holy Trinity.

Holy Week – the seven days between Palm Sunday and Holy Saturday.

Homosexuality – the tendency of some people to prefer sexual relations with members of their own sex.

Hospice – a home for people who are approaching the end of their lives.

I

Icon – a religious painting much valued as an aid for prayer and worship by members of the Orthodox Churches.

Idolatry – the worship of idols instead of God.

Immaculate Conception – the Catholic belief that the Virgin Mary was conceived without Original Sin.

Incarnation – the birth of God (Jesus) on earth.

Indulgence – the doctrine of the Roman Catholic Church that a soul's time in purgatory can be shortened by acts of merit carried out by those still living.

Infant baptism – the anointing of a baby with water so that it becomes a member of the Catholic Church.

J

John the Baptist – the cousin of Jesus who was sent by God to prepare the way for the coming of the Messiah, Jesus.

Just War – the traditional Catholic belief that some wars can be justified on moral grounds.

K

Kingdom of God – the kingdom which God has set up on earth for those who have responded to the teaching of Jesus.

L

Laity – non-ordained members of the Catholic community.

Last Judgement – the Catholic belief that everyone will be called to account for their actions at the end of time when Christ returns to the earth.

Last Supper – the last meal that Jesus shared with his disciples before his crucifixion.

Laying on of hands – the ancient practice of the bishop anointing people to receive the Holy Spirit.

Lent – the time of fasting and spiritual preparation which leads up to Easter. This lasts for a period of 40 days or 6½ weeks (Sundays not counted).

Liturgy – any ordered service of the Church.

Lord's Prayer – the model prayer which Jesus taught his disciples to use.

Lord's Supper – the original term used by St Paul to describe the meal enjoyed by Christians to remember the death of Jesus.

M

Magisterium – the whole teaching ministry of the Catholic Church.

Mass – the central act of Catholic worship – the re-enactment of the sacrifice of Jesus on the cross.

Matrimony – the state of being married.

Maundy Thursday – the day set aside to commemorate the institution of the Eucharist by Jesus Christ.

Meditation – a spiritual discipline often used by catholics in prayer.

Messiah – the 'Anointed One' promised by God to deliver Israel from its enemies. This term was often used to describe Jesus Christ.

Minister – a Free Church priest.

Monastery – the home of a male religious community.

Monk – a member of a male religious community.

N

New Testament – the second part of the Christian Scriptures containing Gospels and Epistles.

Nicene Creed – one of the earliest and most influential of Christian Creeds.

Nun – a member of a religious order of women.

O

Old Testament – the first part of the Christian Bible – books which the Christian Church inherited from its Jewish past.

Oral Tradition – the material which was kept alive by the early Christians by word of mouth before it was written down.

Ordination – the ritual by which lay-people are admitted to the priesthood of the Catholic Church.

Original Sin – the first sin committed by the first man and woman – and passed down to every other human being.

Orthodox Church – the Church which separated from the Roman Catholic Church in the Great Schism of 1054.

Our Father – the Catholic term for the Lord's Prayer.

P

Palm Sunday – the day on which Christians celebrate the entry of Jesus into Jerusalem riding on a donkey.

Papacy – the institution which is headed by the Pope.

Papal Infallibility – the Catholic belief that the Pope speaks infallibly when he is speaking 'Ex Cathedra'.

Parable – a human story which has a moral or a spiritual message.

Paschal Candle – the candle which is lit on Holy Saturday to symbolise the light of Christ's resurrection.

Passover – the annual Jewish festival which commemorates the delivery of the Jews from slavery in Egypt.

Peace – the part of a Roman Catholic service when members of the congregation wish each other 'the peace of God'.

Penance – one of the Church's seven sacraments through which people confess their sins to God through a priest and seek divine forgiveness.

Pentecost – Jewish and Christian festival of the same name.

Pilgrim – someone who undertakes a religious journey to a holy site.

Pill – a contraceptive which alters a woman's hormonal balance and so prevents conception.

Pope – the chief bishop of the Roman Catholic Church and the Bishop of Rome.

Pope John XXIII – the Pope (1958-63) who called the Second Vatican Council

Priest – a man ordained by a bishop to administer the sacraments.

Priesthood – this contains the ordained clergy of the Catholic Church who alone are authorised to administer the sacraments.

Prophet – a man or woman chosen by God to pass on the Divine Word.

Prophets – the books in the Jewish Scriptures which come from such prophetic figures as Isaiah, Jeremiah and Ezekiel.

Protestant – the collective name for those churches which broke away from the Catholic Church during the Reformation.

Psalms – a collection of poems in the Jewish Scriptures written to be sung in worship.

Purgatory – the state after death for those not yet ready for heaven.

Q

Quakers – the religious denomination, also known as the 'Society of Friends', formed in the 17th century by George Fox.

R

Rabbi – a Jewish term for teacher.

Reformation – the movement started in 1517 by Martin Luther which led to the formation of several Protestant Churches.

Relic – the remains of saints or holy people which have become venerated.

Religious Order – an organised group of Christians who have taken vows to live together as a community.

Reserved Sacrament – the keeping back of some of the bread which has been consecrated during the Mass.

Resurrection of the body – the Catholic belief that all true believers will be brought back to life at the end of time.

Revelation – the word used to describe the knowledge which could only be known if God had chosen to make it known.

Roman Catholic Church – the community of believers throughout the world who owe their allegiance to the Pope, Peter's successor.

Rosary – the string of 165 beads used by many Roman Catholics as an aid to prayer.

S

St Francis of Assissi – the founder of the Franciscan religious Order who lived between 1182 and 1226.

St John – one of the disciples of Jesus who wrote the Fourth Gospel and three epistles in the New Testament.

St Paul – early Christian leader who founded many churches and wrote most of the epistles in the New Testament.

St Peter – early Christian leader who undertook missionary journeys and gave his name to two epistles in the New Testament.

Sabbath Day – the Jewish holy day which ran from sunset on Friday to sunset on Saturday.

Sacrament – a physical, material sign of an inward, invisible spiritual blessing.

Saint – a person of outstanding religious commitment – whether alive or dead.

Salvation Army – the Protestant denomination founded by William and Catherine Booth in 1880.

Satan – the 'Accuser' who is seen in the New Testament as the source of all evil.

Second Coming of Christ – the belief that Jesus is going to return to the earth as its judge.

Second Vatican Council – the Council called by Pope John XXIII which met between 1961 and 1965.

Sensus Fidelium – body of faith handed down within the Church from earliest times.

Shrine – originally a place containing the bones of a saint, this now refers to any holy place with religious associations.

Shrove Tuesday – the day before the beginning of Lent when people prepare themselves for the fast ahead.

Sign of the Cross – the tracing of the shape of a cross by a priest or a bishop as a sign of God's blessing.

Soul – the spiritual part of a person.

Speaking in tongues – Praying in a foreign language.

Stations of the Cross – the fourteen places at which, according to the Scriptures and tradition, Jesus stopped on his way to be crucified.

Sterilisation – the operation which makes it impossible for a man to create new life.

Sunday – the 'First Day' of the week which was adopted by the Early Church as a holy day.

Synagogue – a Jewish place of worship.

Synoptic Gospels – the Gospels of Matthew, Mark and Luke which have a similar approach to the life and teaching of Jesus.

T

Tabernacle – a cupboard in a Roman Catholic church, above the altar, in which the Blessed Sacrament is kept.

Ten Commandments – the laws given by God to Moses on Mt Sinai.

Torah – (the Books of the Law) – the first five books of the Jewish Scriptures (Genesis, Exodus, Leviticus, Deuteronomy and Numbers).

Tradition – this is the body of teaching put forward to be believed by all Catholics by Church Councils and Popes.

Transubstantiation – the Catholic belief that the bread and wine become the actual body and blood of Jesus in the Mass.

Trinity – the Christian belief that there are three persons in one God.

V

Viaticum – the name for Holy Communion when it is offered to people who are close to death.

Virgin Birth – the Christian belief that Jesus was miraculously conceived in Mary's womb through supernatural means.

Virgin Mary – the Mother of Jesus Christ who is highly regarded by Catholics.

Vocation – a calling from God to fulfil a particular function.

Votive Candle – these are lit in Church before prayers are offered.

W

Whitsun – the festival, otherwise known as Pentecost, at which the giving of the Holy Spirit is celebrated.

Writings – the third group of books in the Jewish Scriptures alongside the Torah and the Prophets.

INDEX